ABCs

of

ITALIAN WINES

of

ITALIAN WINES

AN ENCYCLOPEDIA

by
JOHN D. SARLES

WINE BOOKS
SAN MARCOS, CALIFORNIA

First Edition

Copyrighted 1981-1979 by John D. Sarles. All rights reserved. Address all inquiries to Wine Books, P.O. Box 1015, San Marcos, CA 92069.

Library of Congress CIP Data:
Sarles, John D,
    ABCs of Italian Wines
80-51642   8010   80030

ISBN   0-9604488-0-2

CONTENTS

GUIDE TO PRONUNICATION OF ITALIAN ALPHABET

A	— ah			I	— ee	
B	— bee			J	— not used	
C	— chee			K	— not used	
		ca	— kah	L	— el-luh	
		ce	— chay	M	— em-muh	
		ci	— chee	N	— en-nuh	
		co	— koh	O	— oh	
		cu	— koo	P	— pea	
D	— dee			Q	— koo	
E	— ay			R	— air-uh	
F	— eff-uh			S	— es-suh	
G	— jee			T	— tea	
		ga	— gah	U	— oo	
		ge	— jay	V	— voo	
		gi	— jee	W	— not used	
		go	— go	X	— not used	
		gu	— goo	Y	— not used	
H	— little used			Z	— zay-tuh	

ACKNOWLEDGEMENTS

Dr. Lucio Caputo, the Italian Trade Commissioner, New York.
Miss Fenella Pearson, Director Italian Wine Promotion Center, New York, and her assistant, Susan Santini.
Mary Ewing Mulligan, Editor U.S. Edition, Italian Wines and Spirits, New York.
Our most devoted tasting group — completely non-professional, who prefer to remain unnamed.
Our many friends who live, and have traveled in Italy, for their contributions.
Innumerable citizens of *Enotria* who have made our trips so pleasant, and furnished material for these pages.
These importers and wholesalers who contributed material:
Thomas B. Abruzzini, New York.
Beccaro International, South San Francisco, CA.
Berisha & Berlinger Imp. Co., New York.
Bonsal Seggerman & Co., New York.
Chambers & Chambers, San Francisco, CA.
De Rosa Vino Co., Kensington, Md.
Domaine Selections, San Rafael, CA.
Dreyfus, Ashby & Co., Los Angeles, CA.
Francis A. Bonnanno, Inc., Miamisburg, Ohio.
G. Raden & Sons, Seattle, Wash.
House of Burgundy, New York.
Mediterranean Importing Co., New Hyde Park, N.Y.
Merchant du Vin, Seattle, Wash.
Musa, Inc., Baltimore, Md.
Pape International, La Grange, Ill.
Paterno Imports, Chicago, Ill.
Palm Bay Imports, Long Island City, N.Y.
Rolar Imports, Great Neck, N.Y.
Spirits of the World, Los Angeles, CA.

For twenty-five years, I have kept voluminous notes on wines from all countries, augmented by those from my own trips and those from friends living in other countries. So far as I know, this is the first attempt in English to collect the specific terms and general information solely on this subject — Italian wines — without technical terms but with related bits of information — using this format.

The subject of wines throughout the world has been treated admirably by many — some of whom may have forgotten more than these pages contain, but as no one has recently seen fit to record the extensive information on these wines in one volume, I felt it a duty and a pleasure to see it accomplished.

A serious back injury in 1976 and the resulting curtailed mobility furnished the catalyst needed to organize this material. That the availability of these wines leaped forward about this time only dictated an increased urgency for this book. The salesman, the storekeeper or wine merchant, the newcomer, the consumer — all will find it a valuable tool as a reference.

John D. Sarles

July 1981

ITALY — LAND OF CONTRASTS!

Spectacularly beautiful mountains — among the highest in the world; wide, clean, shining beaches and the beautiful blue waters encroaching; bleak, arid landscapes that could rival those of our Moon; huge plants and factories among the most modern in the world and tiny farms, each with its group of vines; magnificent Medieval architecture and the round, white-washed houses of the Trulii, as well as the most excellent examples of contemporary architecture; snow and skiing the year 'round in the Alps and the almost unbearable heat of the southernmost area in the summer! Yes, Italy has them all!!

The overall length of the Peninsula is 700 plus miles; the maximum width about 250 miles. The Alps form a distinct barrier from West to East dividing the country from the rest of Europe to the North; the Apennines form a backbone from the Alps south through the "toe of the boot" and into Sicily; actually two-thirds of her landscape is mountainous! Even so, her area of 116,385 square miles* and population of 57 million people produce an incredible eight billion liters of wine from about two million acres of vines in a good year.

ITALY — LAND OF HISTORY!

Long before it was recorded, ancient tribes were settled in the Peninsula according to the archeologists. The Etruscans arrived from Asia Minor (presumably) and settled on the west coast about 1200 BC before the Greeks' and the Carthaginians' first settlements. These early people occupied the area from the Po River on the North to Rome on the South and actually consolidated the several villages of Rome into a City-State about 800 BC. The early Romans drove the Tarquin king from Rome about 510 BC.

---

*The combined areas of Connecticut, Massachusetts, New York, New Jersey and Pennsylvania total 116,011 sq. mi.; that of California is 156,803 sq. mi.

Cato, the eminent Roman who was first a farmer, later a Senator and writer, wrote in detail about agriculture and viticulture in Italy in 150 BC. It was turning into "big business" with more and more acres in vines and fewer in food crops every year. The wines produced were undoubtedly very ordinary, but one can see why Italy today produces and consumes such a tremendous quantity of wines — they have been doing it for over twenty-two centuries — two thousand two hundred years!! And our country has just passed its second centennial!

Pliny the Elder wrote that the first great (?) vintages of Italy appeared about 120 BC and were named OPIMIAN wines in honor of the Roman Consul Opimius. Prior to this, the Greek wines were the favorites of Rome. Pliny also wrote of the tremendous expansion of vineyards and the great demands of the Colonies in France and Germany, giving birth to a new group of business men — the wine brokers — who first opened offices in Lyon, France, during the first century AD.

So much land was planted to the vine that the largest growers (and perhaps the bankers) prevailed upon Emperor Domitian to issue in 92 AD an edict reducing the planting of vines and actually requiring many be removed. This was repealed by Emperor Probus in 280 AD, resulting in another explosion of planting, particularly in France, eventually forcing the wine brokers out of business!

The vine had extended to the Loire Valley in France and into Germany by the 5th Century, but little or nothing was recorded as the world went into the Dark Ages. The Church, which used the product, and the small farmer with a taste for it, are unquestionably responsible for keeping the art alive during the years of invasions by the Goths, Lombards, Franks and others. Charlemagne was crowned Emperor of the Holy Roman Empire in 800 AD and was directly responsible for much planting of the vine in France and Germany.

The beautiful, strong white light of Civilization shown briefly on Italy about 1000 AD. Several universities were founded in the northern and southern cities. Salerno was one city famous as a center of learning for philosophy, theology and medicine. Indeed, one of the first medical schools in the world was founded there by a Greek, a Latin, an Arab and a Jew!!

From 1300 AD, the trade wars among the City-States of Pisa, Genoa, Venice, Amalfi, Florence and Siena were rampant; two invasions from Germany before 1350 bring us to the start of the Renaissance Period and the rise of the merchant class. The main powers at this time were Savoy, the Duchy of Milan, the Republic of Venice, the Republic of Florence, the Papal States and the Kingdom of Naples. Venice for years had confined its energies to the control of trade with the East, but with the fall of Constantinople to the Turks, turned its attention to the mainland.

Pope Urban ended the Great Schism in the Church of Rome and that city was rebuilt as the head of the Papacy in 1455. Another war came with the invasion by Charles VIII of France conquering all of Italy. After his retreat, the Spanish House of Aragon resumed the throne of the Kingdom of Naples. In 1499, Louis XII of France invaded Italy again, with Spain's help, but the Spanish king double-crossed him and set himself up as the King of The Two Sicilies — everything south of Naples including Sicily!

So the same struggles continued — Spain vs. Germany vs. France vs. Austria, with the Pope taking sides as expedient. Net result: Woe to the Land of Wines! The corruption, intrigue, greed, selfishness and dishonesty of all concerned constituted one of the deplorable eras of history. The Treaty of Utrecht (1713) left France "out" of Italy and Austria was "in"; later Phillip V of Spain broke that treaty and invaded. In 1748 after the War of the Austrian Succession, Italy was again divided with France regaining part of it!

For the next forty years, the Land of Wine was fairly quiet, and marked by a decided upturn in internal prosperity, public enterprise, political thought and expression (even a little freedom) under the rulers of that time. Next came Napoleon and his campaigns, and the Treaty of Campo Formio in 1797 ended Venice's independence of 1100 years — Austria getting most of that area. Later the French invaded again, taking Nice and everything south, sacked Rome, forcing the Pope into exile near Paris. After Napoleon was defeated and exiled, the Congress of Vienna in 1815 divided Italy again, returning the Papal States to the Pope — Pius VII.

Freedom raised her bruised head throughout Europe in the ensuing years and many in Italy believed in a unified government for the entire Peninsula; the republicans were jailed, exiled and murdered; the inherent distrust prevented any real progress toward unification until the general uprising across Europe in 1848. Garibaldi, one of the earliest patriots, had been exiled years before. The map on page 8 shows how Italy was partitioned at the start of the Risorgimento, or Unification of Italy. The House of Savoy controlled Piedmont, Liguria, Aosta and Sardinia; Austria controlled everything east of Piedmont, or what we know as Lombardy, Veneto, Trentino-Alto Adige and Friuli-Venezia Giuli. Small areas were known as the Duchy of Parma and the Duchy of Modena; the Republic of Florence was about what we know as Tuscany; the Papal States ruled the area across the middle of the Peninsula and about halfway to Naples from Rome, with the rest of the land south through Sicily under the Spanish Kingdom of The Two Sicilies.

Garibaldi had returned from his exile and in 1860 organized a group of revolutionaries called the "red shirts". With 1000 of them, he invaded Sicily and overwhelmed that island in an incredible ninety days! Flushed with success and 20,000 men, he crossed the Strait of Messina to repeat his feat on the mainland. Count Cavour, the Prime Minister of the House of Savoy (Piedmont, Aosta, Liguria and Sardinia), saw the opportunity for which he had dreamed, and the Piedmont army "blitzed" its way south, by-passed Rome, and joined Garibaldi outside of Naples. Victor Emmanuel II, the head of the House of Savoy and King of Sardinia, was proclaimed King of Italy at Naples in 1861. Garibaldi renounced all of his authority to the new King; Cavour died a few weeks later before he could see his dream completely realized. Later, Venice joined the new country, and in September of 1870, the Italian Army seized Rome and declared it the Capitol of a United Italy! An interesting note: Cavour's successor was a Baron Ricasoli, who has been credited with defining, organizing and instituting the reforms that marked the beginning of the world fame of Chianti!!

3

Most unfortunately there were no statesmen when the new united country so desperately needed leaders. The only universal feeling was distrust — one can readily see why from this short summary of the previous one thousand years! Italy suffered from a succession of weak leaders, a Leftist Parliament, corruption and scandal that prevented her a more honorable place among the nations of the time. In 1900, King Humbert, who had succeeded to the throne in 1878 on the death of Victor Emmanuel II, was assassinated. Victor Emmanuel III became King of Italy.

After the Unification was completed in 1870, southern Italy lost most of its industry to the more progressive, stable and industrious North — which it could little afford. The economy suffered in other ways but with no direction from a central authority and no help from any source, continued to worsen. The climate with its oppressive heat much of the year was not conducive to extreme physical activity. Poverty increased until emigration seemed the only answer. The United States alone took from 50,000 to 350,000 people annually from 1881 to 1910!

Social unrest continued into the opening years of the 20th Century. No strong leaders had yet come forward to guide the nation. Italy tried to stay on the fence in European politics, tried its hand at colonizing parts of Africa when that continent was being "divided" among the European powers, and finally came into World War I on the side of the Allies. The Austro-Hungarian Empire was broken up by the Treaty of Versailles, resulting in the boundaries of Italy almost as we know them today. Minor changes were made after World War II.

While France was not without war for many years, it was unified during the reign of Louis XI, ending in 1483, almost 400 years before Italy. Her days as a world power started under Louis XIV (1643-1715) and her lands scarcely knew an invader for 300 years prior to 1914! The relative stability of her government and her economy, her geographical position on the edge of the Atlantic, and her cultural ties with England and America developed an association that just did not exist with another country. Quite naturally, therefore, Americans looked to France for their wines before and after Prohibition.

ITALY — LAND OF WINES!!

It is next to impossible to trace the origin of the vine and the making of wine; legends, myths and folklore color reality. Many scholars have spent many years in research on this question. In Italy, with its centuries of tradition, this is particularly true. Etruscan tombs dating to 1000 BC reveal that wine was made at that time.

For so many years, most Italians were forced to "look alive to stay alive". Without a common goal and a stable government, and the lack of demand within her own borders, there was no incentive to improve! All the wine produced was consumed by the residents and visitors. One might well remember that Italy, as we know it today, did not exist until five years after our Civil War ended in 1865!

After World War II, millions of dollars were poured into the development of central and southern Italy. Admirable success has been achieved in many places and fields of endeavor. Industry can now be seen where before the barren soil barely supported (?) the people. Much of this money went into the wine industry in those areas to improve the quality and create better and more saleable table wines, instead of the blending wines that went "up North". There will not be too many serious rivals to the magnificent reds of northern Italy, but excellent-to-superior wines are now being made with more on the way.

World opinion, and American opinion, had never been particularly enthusiastic about Italian wines, even if unfairly so. It had, in fact, been quite the opposite. The Common Market brought its share of problems and opportunities — the sharp increase in the prices of French wines on these shores. Suddenly importers were looking for wines to replace the French. Fortunately for us, and for the world, many Italians saw this golden opportunity and lost no time. What sold in Italy does not necessarily sell elsewhere, so their chore was to Clean and Polish their Wine Image!!

The first step: improvement of the wines themselves; large organizations stepped in with the capital necessary for modernizing plants and equipment and methods. The local prejudices that had existed for centuries had to be eliminated where they interfered with the progress of the industry as a whole. Stabilization of wines was a problem to be solved along with many others in producing top-quality wines.

The second step: a wine law with teeth! Such a law was passed in 1963 and is known loosely as the D.O.C. law. It really started a Wine Revolution, or perhaps it could be called a Wine Renaissance! All wines qualifying for D.O.C. status must meet and pass a rather rigid set of requirements AND maintain them. The labels on D.O.C. wines may now be trusted. It is high time the blanket indictment of all wine from Italy is quashed!!

Thus Italy — Land of Contrasts, Land of History, and Land of Wines — is today. Pliny the Elder, listed over 100 wines in his book *Naturalis Historia*, published in the 1st Century AD. There probably are somewhere between 1000 and 2500 wines made today; various writers have estimated as high as 5000. As of July, 1981, there are over 200 zones or areas approved by the D.O.C. committee, covering about 10-12% of the total production. In comparison, France has over 300 A.O.C. wines covering about 10% of their production — which is roughly equal to that of Italy; each produces close to two billion gallons annually.

5

In addition to the 25 or 30 "noble varieties" of grapes grown in France, Germany and California, Italy knows and grows many more; the famous wine school at Conegliano has sponsored a study of grape varieties in Italy that has run to five volumes. Italy is unsurpassed in the variety of wines it produces; was it not Virgil who wrote "He who would know the infinite variety of (Italian) wines would just as well count the grains of sand on the Libyan (Sahara) Desert"?

One of the very great pleasures of Italian wines IS their variety. So often the wines of an area are made for the foods of the area, and isn't that the purpose of wine? There are many, many very good white and red wines, known locally, non-vintaged, that are excellent values and drunk copiously. There are many sparkling wines made all over Italy — each Region has its favorites. Most of the wines over the past twenty years have kept pace with the transition to drier styles, although many are still made *secco, abboccato, amabile,* and *dolce,* or from dry to sweet.

Comparisons with wines of other countries cannot be logical when there are so many differences — variety of grape, soil, climate, etc. If France grew the Nebbiolo grape, then one might check that version of wine with the magnificent Barolo which Italy has made for centuries. On the other hand, the Cabernets, Merlots and Pinot Neros of Italy are producing superior wines in their own styles and cannot be ignored. Under the Common Market regulations, no sugar may be added to any Italian wines because of the greater amount of sunny days to develop the natural grape sugars, yet this is possible under certain conditions in France and Germany, because of less sunshine. (California law also prohibits its use.)

The House of Savoy abdicated the throne in 1946. Under the Constitution (1947) there are now twenty Administrative Regions similar to our states; they are shown on the map on page 9. Most of the Regions are divided into Provinces and many of the Provinces carry the same name as the principal city therein. To avoid confusion, the names of the Provinces are eliminated from this volume. The Regions are:

Abruzzo	Molise
Basilicata	Piemonte (Piedmont)
Calabria	Puglia
Campania	Sardegna (Sardinia)
Emilia-Romagna	Sicilia (Sicily)
Friuli-Venezia Giulia	Toscana (Tuscany)
Lazio	Trentino-Alto Adige
Liguria	Umbria
Lombardia (Lombardy)	Valle D'Aosta
Marche	Veneto (Venezia)

They are listed in alphabetical order in the following pages, each with its map, and giving a few facts interesting to the wine enthusiast.

Italian wines are named in various ways; they may seem confusing because of the many varietal names of grapes used, and the town and area names not being familiar, but they really are quite explicit with the exception of the proprietary or brand names:

1) The name of the grape alone: Albana, Barbera, Greco, Lambrusco, Merlot, Nuragus, Pinot Bianco, Pinot Grigio, Pinot Nero, Riesling Italico, Tocai, etc., etc. See Wine Grape Varieties.

2) The name of the town where the wine is made: Barolo, Carema, Ciro, Donnaz, Frascati, Gambellara, Ghemme, Isonzo, Locorotondo, Marsala, Orvieto, Soave, Sorni, Torgiano, Valgella, etc.

3) A combination of the two names with the grape name first and followed by the name of the town or area from which the grape comes: Barbera d'Asti, Greco di Gerace, Merlot di Pramaggiore, Malvasia de Cagliari, Tocai de Lison, Trebbiano d'Aprilia, etc.

4) A geographical, regional or historical name; there are hundreds of these .wines. When one remembers that Italy was so divided for centuries with fierce local prides, wines, tastes and customs, this is readily understandable. Many of them were never bottled, but were good, inexpensive, satisfying wines made to be drunk before the next harvest. Some of these names are Capri, Castelli Romani, Chianti, Pavese, Toscana Bianco, Verona, Piave, Collio, etc.

5) Proprietary names or brand names: Corvo, Grand Cru, Riunite, Regaleali, etc. There are literally hundreds of these wines. Their names are not included in this volume unless they are well-known and in general distribution, or have achieved a measure of fame for various reasons.

Description of wines in the following pages give the town, or area, in which the wine is made, the Region, and in the case of DOC wines, the percentages of each grape allowed. It should be noted here that these figures are for the percentages of the grape vines IN THE VINEYARD, not for the quantities in the blending vat.

Since history and geography are so interwined with even a cursory study of wines, and the enthusiast's introduction to a wine comes from having read about it or seeing the label, other entries include the geographical, historical and associated words or terms likely to be found on the label. All entries simply add to the reader's general fund of information on Italy and its wines. For these reasons, reproductions of labels are included where possible.

Controversial issues — such as whether a named grape is actually another variety, or sub-variety, or its exact origin or history — are omitted except to report them; the decisions are left to the ampelographers.

A word about the vintage: it is important, but only as a guide! Today there are few, if any, bad years as the technical knowledge will save what would have been a disaster 50 years ago! Of course there are exceptional years, but seldom, if ever, is every wine exceptional in an exceptional year! You may depend on the vintage shown on a DOC label. The suggestions on ages of wines are just that — suggestions! Some vintages will peak later, and a few earlier. Each wine from each winery from each year has a different taste to the professional taster. A fine vintage chart has been prepared by Dr. Antonio Neiderbacher in Milano and is available from the Italian Wine Promotion Center in New York City, or from

ITALY IN 1859

ITALY IN 1981

your own wine merchant. As a general rule, all the Italian white wines are ready to drink as soon as they are bottled, and should be drunk young. The Pinot Biancos, Pinot Grigios, and Tocai wines make excellent aperitif wines along with many other whites. All their white wines are excellent with fish dishes. The rosés and light reds are fine with pork, veal and the lighter meats, including fowl. The full-bodied reds are naturally best with the stronger red meats.

Specific foods or entrees are not included because of the wide variations in foods and their preparation in Italy and here. Few parts of our country serve boar, dove, eel, venison, etc., nor are we as prone to use quantities of olives (oil), anchovies, garlic, and salami in our kitchens (perhaps we should learn!)

Comments, where given, are the concensus of opinion of a group of very intelligent, dedicated, amateur wine lovers. The best advice one can give is still: find a good wine-merchant, trust him, and try his suggestions. Beware of blanket endorsements! The final judge must be, and should be, one's own palate — not forgetting that this, too, will change!

Most of the Italian wines in general distribution in this country are included. The constant improvement in their wines will bring more and more of them to these shores in the future — the total has been growing each year. Figures for 1980 show that 62% of the wines imported into the United States were from Italy for a total of over 54 million gallons! Germany was second with 11.6 million gallons, France third with 11.3 million gallons, and Portugal fourth with 5.6 million gallons. Most of the wines with an appreciable production are listed, as well as the recognized better varieties. The import picture will not stabilize until business firms and tastes stabilize — hence the omission of the names of specific wineries. All brand names are not included as they come and go — the last three years have seen the rise and fall of three or more widely advertised brands in California alone. A basic knowledge of the terms on the labels and characteristics, is, therefore, the responsibility of the good retailer.

The term "candidate for DOC" is used to indicate that that wine may be granted that status. It may mean that the application has been made, or will soon be made, or that approval is about to be announced. Frequently, small problems arise that delay the final approval by the appropriate authorities. For this reason, the reader is referred to page 220 to indicate how he may keep his copy of this volume current; this information will be made available in January of each year.

The Italian Wine Promotion Center at 499 Park Avenue in New York City has done a superb job in its field under the sure guidance of Dr. Lucio Caputo. A magnificent *enoteca* of over 2000 Italian wines was opened in the spring of 1981. Be sure to arrange a visit on your next trip to New York.

So — enough of the intellectual — *nunc est bibendum* (the time to drink is now!!)

ABBOCCATO

(ahb-bohk-KAH-toh)   Slightly sweet or medium-dry; the progression is: *secco* is up to 1% sugar; *abboccato* is from 1% to 2½%; *amabile* is from 2% to 3% sugar; *dolce* is from 3% to 6%.

ABRUZZO

(ah-BROOTZ-tzoh)   One of the twenty Administrative Regions, often mentioned with Molise as they are adjacent; bordered on the N by Marche Region, on the E by the Adriatic Sea, on the S by Molise Region and on the W by Lazio Region; the area is 4,468 square miles, population 1¼ million, the Capitol city L'Aquila; the area was conquered by the Romans in the 4th Century BC, by many others through the centuries, and became part of the Kingdom of Naples after the 13th Century. It is very mountainous, not noted for wine, but there are two DOC wines — Montepulciano d'Abruzzo and Trebbiano d'Abruzzo; these are probably the most widely-planted varieties. The wines were best ignored a decade ago but are changing for the better each year; look for continued improvement and eventually many more to be found in America. The average annual production is about 270 million liters.

ABRUZZO REGION

ACINATO

(ah-chee-NAH-toh)   A sweet dessert wine made near Naples in the Campania Region.

ACINO D'ORO

(AH-chee-no DOHR-oh)   White and rosé wines made in Sicily Region.

ADDA RIVER

(AHD-dah)   rises in the NE corner of Lombardy Region, flows SW then W through Sondrio (the Valtellina area), into the N end of Lake Como, through that lake, joining the Po River W of Cremona; about 150 miles long. Map, page 109.

ADIGE RIVER

(AH-dee-jay)   rises in Austria, flows S into the Trentino-Alto Adige Region and E to Merano, then S through Bolzano, into Veneto Region, through Verona, and in a SE course to the Gulf of Venice N of the Po Delta, About 250 miles. Map, page 187.

AEOLIAN ISLANDS

(ay-OH-lee-an)   The mythological name for the Liparian Islands — off the NE point of Sicily island.

AFFILE

(ahf-FEE-lay)   Small town SE of Rome, Lazio Region, see Cesanese Di Affile.

AGHILOIA

(ah-jee-LOH-ya)   Brand name for a superior wine made from the Vermentino grape in the NE part of Sardinia Region; strong (15%), hard to find, but worth it!

AGLIANICHELLO

(ah-lee-ahn-ee-KEL-loh)   Good red wine made on the island of Procida in the Bay of Naples, Campania Region, from Aglianico and Barbera grapes; ruby-red, semi-dry, varies in taste and body and quality, sometimes has a slight strawberry flavor; best drunk young.

AGLIANICO

(ah-lee-AHN-ee-koh)   Excellent red wine grape grown in several Regions in southern Italy; presumed to be the ancient Greek vine — Hellenica — brought from Greece about 800 BC; used in Taurasi, Vesuvio Rosso, as well as in:

AGLIANICO DEL VULTURE

(ah-lee-AHN-ee-koh del vool-TOO-ray)   **DOC**   Dry, full-bodied, vivid, red-to-garnet wine, full of authority, from Aglianico grapes grown on the sides of Mt. Vulture, an extinct volcano in the N part of Basilicata Region; it must be aged one year before release; with three years (two in wood) it may be labeled *vecchio*, with five years a *riserva*; there is an *amabile* and a sweet *spumante*; peaks about ten. An excellent wine with lamb and pork.

ALBA

(AHL-ba)   City SE of Turin, Piedmont Region, important center of wine trade and the Langhe Hills area.

ALBAN HILLS — ALBANO — ALBANUM

The Alban Hills comprise a beautiful hilly area a few miles S of Rome around Lake Albano; the hills are covered with castles or villas and wines have been made here for thousands of years. The ancient wine here was Albanum.

ALBANA

(ahl-BAH-nah)   Good white wine grape grown in Emilia-Romagna Region.

ALBANA DI ROMAGNA

(ahl-BAH-nah dee roh-MAHN-ya)   **DOC**   This white wine from the Albana grape dates to at least the 14th Century in the Emilia-Romagna Region; straw-yellow to gold, quite fruity with varying degrees of sugar — *secco* or *asciutto*, and *amabile*; fairly heavy yet fresh, a distinctive flavor; good as an aperitif and with fish; the *secco* is recommended; drink at two years, probably before three. This can be an excellent — even a superior wine. A *spumante* is also made.   **DOCG** is imminent.

ALBANA DEL RUBICONE

(ahl-BAH-nah del roo-bee-KOH-nay)   is a white wine made from the Albana grape along the banks of this river in the Emilia-Romagna Region.

ALBANELLO

(ahl-bah-NEL-loh)   White wine grape grown near Syracuse in the Sicily Region, used in:

ALBANELLO DI SIRACUSA

(ahl-bah-NEL-loh dee seer-ah-KOO-sa)   White wine from the Albanello grape near the town of Syracuse in SE Sicily Region; dry, strong (17%), full-bodied, aged for at least five years in the wood.

ALBAROLA

(ahl-bah-ROH-la)   White wine grape grown in the Liguria Region and used in Cinqueterre wine (see).

ALBEROBELLO
(ahl-bair-oh-BEL-loh)   Small town in the Salento Peninsula, Puglia Region, famous for its small, round, one-room, stone houses, constructed without mortar, with conical roofs, dwellings of the Truli, ancient inhabitants of the area.

ALBURNO
(ahl-BOOR-noh)   Good, red wine, dry, produced from Aglianico/Piedirosso/Sangiovese grapes S of Salerno, Campania Region.

ALCAMO or BIANCO ALCAMO
(bee-AHN-koh ahl-KAH-moh)   **DOC**   Either name is allowed. A very good white wine made in the town of Alcamo W of Palermo, Sicily Region, from 80% Catarratto, 20% Trebbiano and other grapes; straw-colored, dry, fresh, fruity, full-bodied, to 14% alcohol; annual production about 150 million liters.

ALEATICO
(ah-lay-AH-tee-koh)   Red wine grape of the Muscat family grown in Lazio, Tuscany, Umbria and Puglia Regions; used in sweet dessert-type wines.

ALEATICO DI BERTINORO
(ah-lay-AH-tee-koh dee bear-tee-NOHR-oh)   An excellent red wine made from the Aleatico grape near the town of Bertinoro in Emilia-Romagna Region; typical Muscat bouquet and flavor.

ALEATICO DI GRADOLI
(ah-lay-AH-tee-koh dee GRAH-doh-lee)   **DOC**   Made from the Aleatico grape in the town of Gradoli about 60 miles N of Rome, Lazio Region; red, sweet and smooth; a *liquoroso* is also made at 17% + and must be aged for six months; typical Muscat bouquet and flavor; peaks about five years.

ALEATICO DI PORTOFERRAIO
(ah-lay-AH-tee-koh dee por-toh-FAIR-yo)   Sweet dessert wine from the Aleatico grape and this town on the island of Elba off the coast of Tuscany Region; ruby-red, smooth, strong, velvety, typically Muscat.

ALEATICO DI PUGLIA
(ah-lay-AH-tee-koh dee POOL-ya)   **DOC**   Good sweet red wine, made all over Puglia Region for at least 100 years, from 85% Aleatico and 15% Negroamaro/Malvasia/Primitivo grapes; there are two types — *dolce naturale*, purple-red, Muscat aroma, smooth and sweet, 15% alcohol, with three years a *riserva*; the other type is a *liquoroso*, 18%, very sweet, also a *riserva* with three years of age; peaks about five or six; small production.

ALEATICO DI TERRACINA
(ah-lay-AH-tee-koh dee tair-rah-CHEE-nah)   Sweet red wine from the Aleatico grape made in the Castelli Romani area, Lazio Region, near the town of Terracina; serve chilled.

ALESSANO

(ahl-ays-SAH-noh) White wine grape grown in Puglia Region; used in making Vermouth and in Martinafranca (see).

ALGHERO

(ahl-GAY-roh) (1) Important city of 32,000 on the W coast of Sardinia Region; excellent port, beautiful beaches, etc. (2) Wines made in the area, many very good, from various grapes including the heavily-grown Cannonau.

ALL'UOVO

(ahl-LWOH-voh) With egg particles; some Marsalas have been made this way for many years. See Marsala.

ALTO ADIGE

(AHL-toh AH-dee-jay) **Ger: SUDTIROLER.** **DOC** The name given to the upper part of the Adige River Basin, roughly from Bolzano N to the Austrian border in the Trentino-Alto Adige Region. For many years the wines were shipped to Germany and Switzerland but with production increasing, we are beginning to get some in this country. All of them are high in quality — from excellent to superior — and must be 95% of the grape named; one exception is the Schiava. Many excellent wine roads in this Region. The second title is the German often seen on the labels in this bilingual area. There are 17 wines:

CABERNET

(ka-bair-NAY) Deep ruby-red, dry, full-bodied, tannic when young, a *riserva* with two years of age; peaks about four.

LAGREIN ROSATO

(lah-GRAIN roh-SAH-toh) **LAGREIN KRETZER** Made from the Lagrein grape; this is a pleasant, light, dry rosé, best drunk in its first year.

LAGREIN SCURO

(lah-GRAIN SKOO-roh) **LAGREIN DUNKEL** The grape is the Lagrein — the wine a ruby-red, dry, fresh, soft and velvety; a *riserva* with one year of age.

MALVASIA
(mal-vah-SEE-ah) **MALVASIER** From the Malvasia grape, a red, sweet, pleasant wine, good with dessert.

MERLOT
(mair-LOH) Red wine from this grape; dry, full-bodied, smooth and soft; a *riserva* with one year of age; drink before five.

MOSCATO GIALLO
(moh-SKAH-toh jee-AHL-loh) **GOLDENMUSKATELLER** Obviously from the Moscato grape — *giallo* is yellow in Italian; straw-colored, sweet, with a typical Muscat bouquet and flavor.

MOSCATO ROSA
(moh-SKAH-toh ROH-sah) **ROSENMUSKATELLER** A rosé made from the Muscat grape, delicate, sweet and pleasant.

PINOT BIANCO
(PEE-noh bee-AHN-koh) **WEISSBURGUNDER** From the Pinot Bianco grape, straw-colored, dry, excellent as an apertif, with much good *spumante* made here from it.

PINOT GRIGIO
(PEE-noh GREE-jee-oh) **RULANDER** Excellent straw-colored, dry, medium-bodied wine from the Pinot Grigiò grape; best in its first year; much good *spumante* made.

PINOT NERO
(PEE-noh NAY-roh) **BLAUBURGUNDER** From the Pinot Nero or Noir grape, deep red with orange tints as it ages, dry, good body, slightly bitter after-taste, a *riserva* with one year, peaks about five.

RIESLING—SYLVANER
(REES-ling sil-VAHN-er) **MULLER-THURGAU** Straw-colored, medium dry, soft, good body, fruity and fresh, good as an aperitif and best in its first year.

RIESLING ITALICO

(REES-ling ee-TAHL-ee-koh) **WELSCHRIESLING** This grape produces a pale-straw wine, dry, light-bodied, fresh tasting.

RIESLING RENANO

(REES-ling ray-NAH-noh) **RHEINRIESLING** This White Riesling grape is slightly different from the one above although both are offshoots from the famous grape. This wine has a little more body than the above, but is not the quality of the famous Rheingau wines.

SAUVIGNON

(soh-veen-YONH) This grape gives an excellent straw-colored, dry, full-bodied wine.

SCHIAVA

(skee-AH-va) **VERNATSCH** The Schiava grape is allowed to be a minimum of 85% with the other 15% local red grapes. The wine is ruby-red, medium-bodied, dry, excellent with red meats and stews, probably best at two-to-three years of age.

SYLVANER

(sil-VAHN-air) The Sylvaner grape produces a straw-colored wine with a greenish tint, light, semi-dry, pleasant carafe wine.

TRAMINER AROMATICO

(trah-MEEN-air ah-roh-MAH-tee-koh) **GEWURZTRAMINER** This grape originated, it is said, in the village of Tramin (Termeno in Italian) in this Region. It is an excellent wine, typical flavor of this grape, medium-bodied, dry.

ALTO SELE

(Ahl-toh SAY-lay) Wines from the upper Sele River valley in the Campania Region; good carafe wines.

ALTRAMURA

(AHL-trah-MOO-rah) A sweet dessert wine made from the Muscat grape in this small town SW of Bari, Puglia Region.

AMABILE

(ah-MAH-bee-lay) Quite sweet — from 2½ to 3% sugar. *Secco* is driest, then *abboccato, amabile* and *dolce.*

AMALFI

(ah-MAHL-fee) City of 6,000 on the Gulf of Salerno, S of Naples, Campania Region, the first of the great Maritime Republics; sacked by Pisa in 1135 and never regained its former glory. There is a beautiful cathedral in the city and the Amalfi Drive is one of THE scenic drives of the world.

AMALFI BIANCO

(ah-MAHL-fee bee-AHN-koh) White carafe wine made around the city of Amalfi, Campania Region, mostly consumed locally.

AMARO
(ah-MAH-roh)   Very dry, bitter.

AMARONE
(ah-mah-ROH-nay)   Dry, rich, red wine, strong (14%), made from *passito* grapes in the Valpolicella area, Veneto Region.

AMBRATO DI COMISO
(ahm-BRAH-toh dee koh-MEE-soh)   White wine from Catarratto and Inzolia grapes, amber in color, dry, strong (14%), sometimes sweet, made E of Ragusa in the SE tip of Sicily Region. Very small production, but a candidate for D.O.C.

AMELIA
(ah-MAYL-ya)   Town W of Terni in the S part of Umbria Region producing good red wines from the Sangiovese and good whites from the Trebbiano; mostly consumed locally.

AMPOLLA DA GHIACCIO
(ahm-POHL-lah da gee-ACH-choh)   A glass decanter blown with a pocket in the side to hold ice to chill the wine — a good conversation piece! Some Chianti is shipped to this country in these containers.

ANCONA
(ahn-KOH-nah)   Port City of 113,000 on the Adriatic Sea and Capitol of the Marche Region.

ANGERA
(ahn-JAY-rah)   Very good red wine from the Barbera and other grapes produced around this small town on the SE side of Lake Maggiore, Lombardy Region.

ANGHELU RUJU
(AHN-gay-loo ROO-yoo)   Brand name for an unusual red, slightly sweet wine, made from the Cannonau grape near Alghero in Sardinia Region; smooth, velvety, strong (17%), very well-rounded; the *passito* grapes give it a spicy, rich, nutty flavor; better with three or four years of age. The name is translated "red angel."

ANNATA

(ahn-NAH-tah)   Year.

ANSONICA

(ahn-SOH-nee-kah)   Good white carafe wine made from the Trebbiano grape and others, in the Tuscany Region; straw-colored, fresh tasting, made both *secco* and *amabile.*

AOSTA

(ah-OH-sta)   City of 20,000 and Capitol of the Valle d'Aosta Region; founded about 25 BC as the Roman colony Augusta Pretoria.

APRILIA

(ah-PREE-lee-ya)   Town and area S of Rome in Lazio Region, in what was known for centuries as the Pontine Marshes. Drained in the 1930s, the area is now producing excellent to superior wines, several with D.O.C. status.

APULIA

(ah-POOL-ya)   See Puglia.

AQUILA

See L'Aquila. Not to be confused with the following:

AQUILEIA

(ah-KWEE-lay-yah)   **DOC**   Small town 20 miles S of Udine near Trieste in the Friuli-Venezia Giulia Region; named for a Roman fort built there *c.* 185 BC. Wines have been made there since then but mostly consumed locally until recent increases in producton make them more widely available. They are excellent-to-superior in quality. The varietal name appears on the label and the wine must be 90% of that variety; there are seven:

CABERNET

(kah-bair-NAY)   Either the Cabernet Franc or the Cabernet Sauvignon grape may be used with 10% other reds; deep ruby-red, dry, full-bodied, needs age; an excellent wine good for 8-10 years. Best with good red meats, naturally.

MERLOT
(mair-LOH)   The Merlot grape produces an excellent-to-superior red wine, dry, soft and velvety; peaks about five.

PINOT BIANCO
(PEE-noh bee-AHN-koh)   Excellent white wine from the Pinot Bianco grape, dry, fresh-tasting, full-bodied, best when young.

PINOT GRIGIO
(PEE-noh GREE-joh)   Another excellent white wine from the Pinot Grigio grape; dry, soft, medium-bodied, good as an aperitif and best when young.

REFOSCO
(ray-FOH-skoh)   The Refosco grape produces a deep ruby-red, sturdy, full-bodied wine, with a slightly bitter after-taste, better with a little age.

RIESLING RENANO
(REES-ling ray-NAH-noh)   Very good white wine from the White Riesling grape; pale gold, dry, medium-bodied.

TOCAI FRIULANO
(toh-KIE free-oo-LAH-noh)   This grape, at home in this Region, produces an excellent white, dry, well-balanced wine in this zone — one of the best from this grape.

ARBIA RIVER
(AHR-bee-ah)   A river in Tuscany Region — S of the Chianti *classico* area. Good white wines from the Trebbiano and other grapes are made in the area.

ARDENGHESCA
(ahr-den-GAY-ska)   Excellent white wine from the area near Grosseto (the Maremma) in the SW part of Tuscany Region; 75-80% Trebbiano, 20% Malvasia grapes, straw-yellow, dry, delicate; drink it young.

ARNEIS
(ahr-NAY)   An excellent white wine grape formerly heavily grown in Piedmont Region but it has almost disappeared with the heavy emphasis on fine red wines; it produces a dry, fruity wine with a slight bitter-almond flavor; hard to find as the production is quite small.

ARNO RIVER
(AHR-noh)   rises in the E part of Tuscany Region, flowing in a big U-shape through Florence, W through Pisa into the Tyrrhenian Sea, about 155 miles long.

ASCIUTTO
(ah-SHOOT-toh)   Very dry, drier than *secco*, but not bitter like *amaro*.

ASPRINIO
(ah-SPREEN-yoh)   White wine grape of mediocre quality rather high in acid, grown in the Basilicata, Campania and Lazio Regions.

ASPRINIO DELL'AVERSANO
(as-SPREEN-yoh del-lah-vair-SAHN-oh)   White carafe wine from the Asprinio grape made near Naples, Campania Region, light and dry, quite high in acid usually.

ASTI
(AH-stee)   City of 80,000 people SE of Turin in Piedmont Region, famous as the home of Asti Spumante wines.

ASTI SPUMANTE
(AH-stee spoo-MAHN-tee)   **DOC**   Asti is the name of the town and *spumante* is Italian for sparkling. The entire world knows this fine, sweet, pale wine made from the Muscat grape by the Charmat process (fermented in the vat instead of in the bottle); it has about 5% sugar, typical Muscat bouquet and flavor, must be served very cold. There is also a Kosher Asti Spumante made. Total annual production is about fifty million liters. See Moscato D'Asti for more explanation.

AVANAT
(ah-vahn-AHT)   Red wine grape grown in western Piedmont Region and the dry, full-bodied wine made from it — consumed locally.

AVELLINO
(ah-vel-LEEN-oh)   Small city about 30 miles E of Naples, Campania Region, the center of much wine production; the area suffered extensive damage in the 1980 earthquake.

AYMAVILLE
(Fr: ah-may-VEE-yuh)   Small town in the Aosta Valley (and Region) and the red wine made there; dry, smooth, full-bodied, from the Petit Rouge grape.

AZIENDA AGRICOLA
(ahtz-ee-en-da ah-gree-KOH-la)   A firm engaged in agriculture.

21

BACCO

B

BACCANALE

(bahk-kah-NAH-lay) (1) Good white carafe wine made and consumed in the Alban Hills area near Rome, Lazio Region. (2) Red wine from Cesanese/Cabernet Franc/Carignane made dry and semi-dry N of Rome near Lake Braciano.

BACCO

(BAHK-koh) Italian god of wine; Bacchus was the Roman god of wine and the Greek god of wine after about 1000 BC; prior to that time the name Dionysus appears more often.

BALESTRIERE

(bal-ESS-tree-air-uh) An odd name meaning "cross-bowman" for a favorite red wine in the Lombardy Region; probably a mixture of Barbera and Bonarda grapes from the area S of the Po River — the Oltrepò Pavese.

BALLOTTA

(bahl-LOHT-tah) Brand name for red, white and rosé wines made in Sicily Region.

BARBACARLO

(bar-bah KAHR-loh) **DOC** part of the Oltrepò Pavese zone, Lombardy Region; red wine from Barbera/Uva Rara/Ughetta grapes, dry, good body, one year of wood aging is required; some tasters find a trace of raspberry.

BARBARESCO *10-3-80*

(bar-bar-ESS-koh) ~~DOC and a candidate for~~ DOCG A superior red wine made from the Nebbiolo grape around this town in Piedmont Region; lighter, softer and shorter-lived than its famous cousin — the Barolo — but still a very distinguished wine that has much in common with Barolo; deep ruby-red showing an orange tint with age, dry, full-bodied, well-balanced; two years of age (one in wood) required before release, with three years, a *riserva*; with four years a *riserva speciale*; annual production is about two million liters; normally at its best at from three to six years; for the best red meats.

BARBAROSSA

(bar-bar-OHS-sah)   Red wine made from Barbarossa grapes in the W part of Liguria Region; light, dry, interesting taste, sometimes *frizzante*; a *rosato* also made; named after the Emperor Frederick of Barbarossa; very limited production.

BARBERA

(bar-BEAR-ah)   Excellent red wine grape and the wine, native of the Asti area of Piedmont Region but grown in several other Regions as well; probably the closest to the everyday wine of many northern Italians. Cellar treatment varies to produce all the versions − *secco, abboccato, amabile, frizzante, spumante, rosato* and even a white! Over 200 million liters produced annually; the average wine peaks at from three to five years.

BARBERA D'ALBA

(bar-BEAR-ah DAHL-bah)   **DOC**   From the Barbera grape and the town of Alba in Piedmont Region, this wine allows 15% Nebbiolo grapes; deep red when young with a purple tint as it ages, slightly tannic, dry, full-bodied, well-rounded, must have two years of age (one in wood) before release, probably at its best from three to five years; a *superiore* and an *amabile* are available. There are about 4 million liters made annually.

BARBERA D'ASTI

(bar-BEAR-ah DAHS-tee)   **DOC**   This red wine is 100% Barbera grapes from around the city of Asti, Piedmont Region, and reputed to be the best of the Barbera wines; deep ruby-red in its youth with purple tints developing as it ages, must have two years of age (one in wood) before release; probably best at from four to six years; a *superiore* and an *amabile* are allowed; annual production about 20 million liters.

BARBERA D'AVELLINO

(bar-BEAR-ah dah-vel-LEEN-oh)   Excellent red wine, dry and full bodied, from the Barbera grape made near Avellino, Campania Region; considered by some connoisseurs to be superior to the Piedmont Barberas!

BARBERA DEI COLLI PIACENTINI

(bar-BEAR-ah day KOHL-lee pee-ah chen-TEE-nee) Excellent Barbera wine from the hills S of Piacenza in Emilia-Romagna Region where it has been nominated for DOC; it is dry, full-bodied and peaks about five.

BARBERA DEI COLLI TORTONESI

See Colli Tortonesi.

BARBERA DEL MONFERRATO

(bar-BEAR-ah del mohn-fair-RAH-toh) **DOC** Must be made from 75-90% Barbera grapes with the balance of Dolcetto/Freisa/Grignolino in the Monferrato area of Piedmont Region; made both *secco* and *amabile* and *frizzante*; generally lighter than the other Piedmont Barberas; with two years of age a *superiore*; at its best from three to seven years. Annual production is about five million liters.

BARBERA DEL PARMENSE

(bar-BEAR-ah- del par-MAIN sa) Another very good Barbera wine from the city of Parma in Emilia-Romagna Region; red, dry, full-bodied and a candidate for DOC.

BARBERA DEL SANNIO

(bar-BEAR-ah-del-SAHN-nee-oh) From the Barbera grape and the town of Sannio, NE of Avellino in Campania Region; this wine is a little stronger and both *secco* and *amabile*.

BARBERA DELL'OLTREPO PAVESE
See Oltrepò Pavese.

BARBERA DI LINERO
(bar-BEAR-ah dee lee-NAIR-oh)   Very good wine from the Barbera grape made near Linero in the SE corner of the Liguria Region; deep-red, dry, full-bodied; drink before it is five.

BARI
(BAR-ee)   Port and Capitol city of the Puglia Region; a fine cathedral, museum and university in this city of 175,000 on the Adriatic coast.

BARDOLINO
(bar-doh-LEEN-oh)   **DOC**   One of Italy's best-known wines from the town of this name and the area around it at the SE tip of Lake Garda in Veneto Region. The grapes are 50-65% Cortina, 10-30% Rondinella, 10-20% Molinara, to 10% others; dry, medium-red, light-to-medium body, excellent luncheon and picnic wine; at its best when fresh — avoid it if over four; the *classico* zone is next to the town and there is also a *superiore*; annual production is about 15 million liters.

BARDOLINO CHIARETTO
(bar-doh-LEEN-oh key-AHR-ET-toh)   is a rosé, excellent when young and fresh, superior to many of the rosés of the world.

BAROLO
(bar-OH-lo)   **DOC**   Unquestionably one of the finest red wines of the world — with proper aging; Barolo is made from the Nebbiolo grape and takes its name from the small town in Piedmont Region. Harsh when young, three years of age is required, four for a *riserva*, five for a *riserva speciale*; at its best at from 10 to 15 years of age when it is rich, majestic, full-bodied and magnificent; sometimes throws a sediment. The best vintages will live for 20 + years before peaking. Various tasters find traces of violets, tar and roses in this wine; also allowed is a mixture of *Chinato* in Barolo, resulting in a bitter aperitif. The annual production is from 5 to 6 million liters; it is best to let it breathe for from 2 to 6 hours depending on its age.

BASILICATA

(bah-see-lee-KAH-tah)   This Region is the "arch of the boot" — bounded on the N and E by Puglia, touching the Ionian Sea, on the S by Calabria, a few miles of the Tyrrhenian coast but mostly Lazio on the west. It is about 3850 square miles of bleak, barren land inhabited by 600,000 people; the Capitol city is Potenza in the north central part — an area that sustained heavy damage in the earthquake of November 1980. The ancient Greek name was Lucania after the ancient inhabitants — the Lucanii. The Romans conquered it in the 3rd Century BC and after them the Lombards, Byzantine Empire, the Normans and later the Kingdom of Naples. One claim to fame is that Venosa was the birthplace of Horace. The wine production is about 45 million liters annually with Aglianico Del Vulture the only DOC wine at this point.

BASILICATA REGION

BASSO SELE

(BAHS-soh SAY-la)   Wines from the lower part of the Sele River valley in the S part of the Campania Region.

BELL'AGIO

(bel-LAH-gee-oh)   Brand name for a light, medium-dry, pleasant white wine produced at the W end of Sicily Region.

BELLONE

(bel-LOHN-ay)   White wine grape grown in the Lazio Region.

BERTINORO

(bear-tee-NOHR-oh)   Small town S of Imola in the Emilia-Romagna Region, and its excellent white wine made from the Albana grape; dry, fruity and delicate; an *amabile* is made and also a sweet dessert type.

BIANCHELLO

(bee-ahn-KEL-loh)   Good white wine grape grown in the Marche Region, aka Biancame.

BIANCHELLO DEL MATAURO

(bee-ahn-KEL-loh-del mah-TOR-oh)   **DOC**   Excellent white wine from the Bianchello grape grown in the Matauro valley in the Marche Region; very dry, almost flinty, fresh, well-balanced, fruity, excellent with fish; drink it young. This wine has been tremendously improved in the last ten years; annual production about 750,000 liters.

BIANCO

(bee-AHN-koh)   White, in Italian. *Vino Bianco* is any white wine; there are hundreds of these made all over Italy, using the grapes at hand — some ordinary, some good, some excellent, and varying from dry to sweet — whatever will sell locally.

BIANCO ALCAMO or ALCAMO

(bee-AHN-koh ahl-KAHM-oh)   or ALCAMO   **DOC**   Very good white wine made around the town of Alcamo W of Palermo, Sicily Region; from 80% Catarratto, 20% Trebbiano and other grapes; straw-colored, dry, fresh, fruity, full-bodied, to 14%; annual production about 150 million liters.

BIANCO CAPENA

(bee-AHN-ko kah-PAY-nah)   **DOC**   Good white wine from 55% Malvasia, 25% Trebbiano, to 20% Bellone/Bombino grapes, made near the town of Capena, N of Rome, Lazio Region; both *secco* and *amabile* are made with a *superiore* available.

BIANCO COLLI EMPOLESI

(bee-AHN-ko KOHL-lee AYM-poh-LAY-see)   An excellent white wine from Trebbiano and Malvasia grapes made in the hills around the old city of Empoli about 30 miles from Florence, Tuscany Region.

BIANCO D'ENOTRIA

(bee-AHN-koh day-NOH-tree-ah)   Brand name for a good white wine made from Greco/Malvasia grapes not far from the Ciro area in Calabria Region.

28

BIANCO DEI COLLI APUANI

(bee-AHN-ko day KOHL-lee ah-poo-AH-nee) White wine made from 60-70% Vermentino and the balance of Procanico/Greco grapes; both *secco* and *amabile* available. The area is the NW tip of Tuscany Region not too far from the hills producing the Carrara marble. Candidate for DOC.

BIANCO DEI COLLI MACERATESI

(bee-AHN-ko day KOHL-lee mah-chay-rah-TAY-see) **DOC** From the hills around Macerata in the Marche Region comes this dry, well-balanced good carafe wine, made from 50% Trebbiano, 30-50% Maceratino and to 15% Verdicchio/Malvasia grapes.

BIANCO DEI ROERI

(bee-AHN-ko day ROAR-ee) The Nebbiolo grape is used in this white wine made in the Roeri Hills N of Alba in the Piedmont Region, generally clean, crisp and dry. It is also made with some Arneis grape with the Nebbiolo.

BIANCO DEL MOLISE

(bee-AHN-ko del moh-LEE-sa) Good white wine from Bombino and other grapes made in the Molise Region. Candidate for DOC. There is also a Rosso Del Molise (see).

BIANCO DELLA LEGA

(bee-AHN-ko del-la LAY-ga) A new entry on the white wine scene resulting from the prohibition of White Chianti under DOC, made from the Trebbiano and Malvasia grapes under rules set by the Chianti Classico consortium, and limited to that area, in Tuscany Region. It is possible that other grapes and wines may be added. Candidate for DOC. See Galestro.

BIANCO DELLA VALDELSA

(bee-AHN-koh del-la vahl-DEL-sa) Very good white wine, basically a Trebbiano, made in the Elsa River valley near Florence, in Tuscany Region. Candidate for DOC.

BIANCO DELLA VALDINIEVOLE

(bee-AHN-ko del-la vahl-dee-nee-AY-voh-lay) **DOC** This white wine is made from 70% Trebbiano, 25% Malvasia/Canaiolo/Vermentino grapes, straw-yellow to gold, dry, strong grape flavor. A *rosso* is made, but not DOC.

BIANCO DI CANDIA

(bee-AHN-ko dee KAHN-dee-ah) This proposed zone, a candidate for DOC, is a valley near the Carrara marble country, in the NW part of Tuscany Region. The vineyards are terraced and require hand labor to produce the wine in this very old area. It is made from 60-70% Vermentino grapes with Procanico and Greco for the balance; both a *secco* and an *amabile* are made.

BIANCO DI CASTELFRANCO

(bee-AHN-koh dee kahs-tel-FRAHN-ko) White wine made in this town a few miles SE of Modena in the Emilia-Romagna Region; probably from the Trebbiano grape plus others; candidate for DOC.

BIANCO DI CUSTOZA

(bee-AHN-ko dee koo-STOH-tzah) **DOC** Excellent white wine made near the town of Custoza in Veneto Region; the grapes are 20-30% Garganega, 20-30% Cortese/Malvasia/Riesling Italico, 35-55% Trebbiano, 5-15% Tocai; one can see why it may vary in taste; straw-colored, dry, aromatic, slightly bitter after-taste; a *spumante* is made. Custoza was an ancient Roman outpost or fort.

BIANCO DI LINERO

(bee-AHN-koh dee lee-NAIR-oh) Good white wine, dry, medium-bodied, made in Liguria Region; drink it young.

BIANCO DI MAREMMA

(bee-AHN-ko dee may-RAYM-ma) Maremma is the coastal plain from Pisa to Grosseto on the W side of Tuscany Region. This wine is basically a Trebbiano but Ansonica is also used; very good, dry, slightly bitter, excellent as an aperitif, but best drunk young and cool.

BIANCO DI OSTUNI

See Ostuni.

BIANCO DI PITIGLIANO

(bee-AHN-ko dee pee-tee-lee-YAH-noh) **DOC** An excellent light- to medium-bodied wine from 65-70% Trebbiano, 30-35% Greco grapes made near the town of Pitigliano in the S part of Tuscany Region; straw-yellow, soft, dry, drink it young.

BIANCO DI SCANDIANO

(bee-AHN-ko dee skahn-dee-AH-no) **DOC** Excellent white wine made in the town of Scandiano, Emilia-Romagna Region, from 85% Sauvignon, 15% Malvasia/Trebbiano grapes; cellar treatment varies to give a *secco, abboccato, amabile, frizzante* and *spumante*; the *secco* is preferred.

BIANCO GRANATELLO

(bee-AHN-ko grahn-ah TEL-lo) Brand name for a good white wine made from Catarratto and other grapes in the Sicily Region.

BIANCO PISANE DI SAN TORPE

(bee-AHN-ko pee-SAHN-uh dee sahn TOR-pay) **DOC** Excellent white wine from 70% Trebbiano, to 30% Canaiolo Bianco/Malvasia grapes, made near Pisa, Tuscany Region; straw-colored, dry, slightly bitter after-taste.

BIANCO TOSCANA

(bee-AHN-ko toh-SKAHN-ah) A generic name for much of the ordinary-to-good-to-fine white wine — most of it with a Trebbiano base, made all over the Region of Tuscany; much of it was formerly labeled Chianti Bianco.

BIANCO TRIGLIA

(bee-AHN-ko TREE-lee-ya) Brand name for a good white wine made from Grecanico/Catarratto grapes in the Sicily Region.

BIANCO VERGINE VALDICHIANA

(bee-AHN-ko vair-JEEN-ah vahl-dee-key-AH-na) **DOC** From the Chiana Valley S of Arezzo in Tuscany Region, this is an excellent white wine made from 70-85% Trebbiano, 10-20% Malvasia and other grapes; straw-colored, semi-dry, medium-bodied, slightly bitter after-taste. The good red wines made here are not DOC.

31

BIANCOLELLA
(bee-AHN-koh-LEL-lah)   Good white wine grape grown heavily on the islands of Capri and Procida in the Bay of Naples, Campania Region; the wine made from it is light yellow, dry, a pleasant carafe wine.

BIBLINO
(bee-BLEE-noh)   Pliny wrote of this wine made in Sicily and presumed to be from the Moscato grape.

BICCHIERE DA VINO
(beek-kee-YAIR-ay dah VEE-no)   A wine glass.

BIELLA
(bee-YEL-lah)   Red wine made in Piedmont Region.

BIRGI
(BEER-jee)   Brand name for a strong (16%), white wine made in Sicily Region. There is also a red wine made there.

BLANC DE MORGEX ET DE LA SALLE
(Fr: blawn dee mohr-JEX ay dee la sahl)   The name of the grape is the Blanc de Morgex and also known as Valdigne; it is grown around these two towns in the Val D'Aosta Region and said to be the ancestor of the White Riesling. The vineyards are at 3000' and the wine has been made there since the 13th Century; pale-to light-gold, light, dry, fresh, famous for its taste of Alpine flowers; best drunk young. An interesting note: these vineyards escaped the phylloxera in its ravages of European vineyards! About 50,000 liters made annually. Candidate for DOC.

BLAUBURGUNDER
German name for the Pinot Nero (Pinot Noir) grape in the Trentino-Alto Adige Region.

BOBBIO
(BOHB-bee-oh)   Red wine made in the Piedmont Region.

BOCA
(BOH-kah) **DOC** Superior red wine from the town of Boca in the Novara Hills area of Piedmont Region; made from 45-70% Nebbiolo, 20-40% Vespolina, to 20% Bonarda grapes; harsh when young but softens and improves considerably with age; ruby-red, dry, complex, full-bodied, must be three years old (two in wood) before release, but much better with ten years behind it. Annual production about 15,000 liters.

BOLOGNA
(boh-LOHN-ya) City and Capitol of the Emilia-Romagna Region, 500,000 population, sometimes called the "Gourmet Capitol of the World." An important center for learning since Medieval times; built on the site of an Etruscan city — Felsina; the University was started in the 11th Century; much fine historical architecture including many churches. Be sure to visit the *Enoteca Di Bologna* — a choice display of some 1200 Italian wines.

BOLZANO
(bohl-TZAH-noh) City of 100,000 population in the N part of Trentino-Alto Adige Region; known under the Austrian occupation as Bozen which often appears on wine labels; for wines, see Alto Adige and Terlano.

BOMBINO
(bohm-BEE-no) Two wine grapes, *bianco* and *nero*, grown extensively in Puglia Region; the wine made from them is used as a blending wine.

BONARDA
(boh-NAHR-da) Good red wine grape and the wine made from it in the Novara Hills area of Piedmont Region; ruby-red, light to medium body, dry, pleasant aroma, best when young and slightly chilled. One extensive use of this grape is to soften the Nebbiolo; also grown extensively in the Oltrepò Pavese (see) area of Lombardy Region and said to be the same grape as the Croatina.

BONARDA AMABILE
(boh-NAHR-da ah-MAH-bee-lay) Red, fairly sweet wine from the Bonarda grape made all over Lombardy Region.

BONVINO
(bohn-VEE-no) White wine grape grown in the Alban Hills S of Rome, Lazio Region; used in the wines in the area — Colli Lanuvini, Marino and others.

BORGOGNA BIANCO and **BORGOGNA NERO**
Local German names in the Alto Adige area for the Pinot Bianco (Pinot Blanc) and the Pinot Nero (Pinot Noir); the Region is Trentino-Alto Adige.

BOSA
(BOH-sah) Small town in Sardinia Region famous for its Malvasia (see).

BOSCO
(BOH-skoh) White wine grape grown in Liguria Region; used in Cinqueterre and other wines.

BOSCO ELICEO

(BOH-skoh ey-lee-CHAY-oh) Red wine from Uva d'Oro grapes made from Ravenna N to the Po River, Emilia-Romagna Region; ruby-red, dry, sometimes tannic, light-bodied, and only about 10% alcohol. It is better when served cool and with the lighter meats; varies in taste among wineries. Candidate for DOC.

BOTTE

(BOHT-tay) Barrel.

BOTTICINO

(boht-tee-CHEE-no) **DOC** Superior red wine from the town of Botticino E of Milan, Lombardy Region; made from 30-40% Barbera, 20-30% Schiava, 15-25% Marzemino, 10-20% Sangiovese; dry, quite robust, tannic when young, but nicely balanced with age; about 200,000 liters produced annually.

BOTTIGLIA

(boht-TEE-lee-yuh) Bottle.

BOVALE

(boh-VAHL-ay) Red wine grape grown in Sardinia Region; used in Campidano di Terralba and other wines.

BOZEN

(BOH-tzen) Austrian name for the city now called Bolzano, Trentino-Alto Adige Region.

BRACHETTO

(brah-KAYT-toh) Good red wine grape grown heavily in Piedmont Region, and the wine made from it, often with a little Moscato in it; much *spumante* made; drink it young.

BRACHETTO D'ACQUI

(bray-KAYT-toh DAH-kee) **DOC** Good red wine made from 90% Brachetto and 10% Aleatico (red Muscat) grapes, in and near the town of Acqui in Piedmont Region; medium red, Muscat aroma, slightly bubbly, made both *secco* and *amabile*, also an excellent *spumante*. Over one million liters made annually but not all DOC.

BRAMATERRA

(brah-mah-TAIR-rah) **DOC** Excellent red wine from the hills NW of Novara in Piedmont Region; from 50-70% Nebbiolo, with the balance from Croatina or Bonarda and Vespolina; red with orange tints as it ages, dry, full-bodied, and smooth with proper age — two years is required; a *riserva* with three years. Peaks about ten years; drink it with red meats.

BREGANZE

(bray-GAHN-tzay)   **DOC**   Breganze is a small town N of Vicenza in Veneto Region and lends its name to this zone for six wines:

BIANCO

(bee-AHN-koh)   white-to-gold, dry, full-bodied wine from 85% Tocai and 15% others; best when young.

CABERNET

(kah-BAIR-nay)   Made from either the Cabernet Franc or the Cabernet Sauvignon grape; red, dry, full-bodied; a *superiore* is available; peaks about five.

PINOT   BIANCO

(PEE-noh bee-AHN-koh)   Made from 40-60% Pinot Bianco and 60-40% Pinot Grigio grapes; light, straw-colored, smooth and soft; a *superiore* is available; drink it young.

PINOT   NERO

(PEE-noh NAY-roh)   100% Pinot Nero grapes produce here a ruby-red, dry, full-bodied wine; it is smoother with a little age but drink before five; a *superiore* is available.

ROSSO

(ROHS-soh)   Good, dry, red wine, smooth, soft and ready to drink early, as it is made from 85% Merlot and 15% other grapes, peaks at four or five. Serve with red meats.

VESPAIOLO

(vays-pah-YEE-OH-lo)   Made from the Vespaiolo grape, this wine is golden in color, dry and full-bodied; a *superiore* is available.

BRESCIA

(BRAY-sha)   City of 215,000 near the SW end of Lake Garda, Lombardy Region; important wine trade center.

BRINDISI

(BREEN-dee-see) **DOC** Port city and Italian Naval Base on the Adriatic side of the Salento Peninsula, Puglia Region; there is no *bianco* in the DOC:
ROSATO
(roh-SAH-toh) is made from Negroamaro/Red Malvasia/Montepulciano/ Sangiovese grapes; fruity and dry; a very good rosé.
ROSSO
(ROHS-soh) is also made from Negroamaro/Red Malvasia/Montepulciano/Sangiovese grapes; ruby-red, dry, smooth, slightly bitter after-taste; a *riserva* is available.

BRUNELLO

(broo-NAYL-lo) Red wine grape related to the Sangiovese grown in Tuscany Region, producing the famous Brunello Di Montalcino; and from younger vines — Rosso dai Vigneti, etc.

BRUNELLO DI MONTALCINO

(broo-NAYL-loh dee mohn-tal-CHEE-noh) **DOC** and **DOCG** A superb red wine made from the Brunello grape and carrying the name of this small town in the Siena Hills of Tuscany Region. One of Italy's finest red wines and must be counted among the world's great wines; ruby-red, dry, tannic when young, an intense aroma, aged four years in wood before release, with five years a *riserva*; with proper care, will live for fifty or more! Truly a magnificent wine; about 1½ million liters made annually. It often needs 24 hours breathing time. See also Rosso dai Vigneti.

BUTTAFUOCO

(boot-tah-FWOH-koh) **DOC** An odd name meaning "spitfire" for a very good red wine made in the Oltrepò Pavese (and part of the DOC group), Lombardy Region; made from Uva Rara, Bonarda and Barbera grapes; dry, well-rounded, medium-bodied, best drunk young.

BUZZETTO

(bootz-TZET-toh) A good white wine from the Lumassina grape made near Quiliano in Liguria Region; straw-yellow, fresh-tasting, dry, light-bodied; drink it in the first year.

CABERNET DEL PIAVE
See Vini Del Piave.

CABERNET DI PRAMAGGIORE
(kah-bear-NAY dee prah-mahj-JOHR-ay)   **DOC**   An excellent-to-superior red wine from this grape and the area around the town of Pramaggiore in Veneto Region, N of Venice; made from 90% Cabernet Franc and 10% Merlot, deep, ruby-red, dry, full-bodied, well-balanced, needs age for best results; a *riserva* is available; peaks about 6-8 years. A new zone to be called Lison-Pramaggiore (see) when approved, will include this wine.

CABERNET FRANC and **CABERNET SAUVIGNON**
These two superior red wine grapes were introduced into Italy prior to 1820 and at one time grew almost all over the Peninsula; the growing areas today are mostly the NE and N sections although some experimental plantings are farther south. It is presumed that universal plantings were abandoned because of the low yield from the vine. With the continued emphasis on wines of superior quality, there has been much experimentation in the last ten years with some surprising results: Veneto, Tuscany and Emilia-Romagna are producing some superb wines. See also Fiorano, Carmignano, Mori Vecio, Sassicaia and Tignanello.

CACC'E MMITTE DI LUCERA

(KAH-chay MEET-tay dee-loo-CHAIR-ah) **DOC** Lucera is a small town five miles NW of Foggia, Puglia Region; "Cacc'e Mmitte" can be translated "pour it and drink it"; the grapes are 35-60% Uva Di Troia, 25-35% Montepulciano/Sangiovese/Malvasia, 15-30% Trebbiano/Bombino/Malvasia; with this complicated formula, the resulting wine will vary in taste; it is generally deep red, full-bodied and needs age to soften.

CAFARO

(kah-FAHR-oh) Small village in Calabria Region producing a very deep red wine, strong, both dry and semi-dry — mostly consumed locally.

CAGLIARI

(KAHL-yar-ee) Port city of 250,000 population on the S end of the island and the Capitol of the Sardinia Region; founded by the Carthaginians about 800 BC, center of wine trade.

CAGNINA

(kahn-YEE-na) Very good red wine from the Terrano grape made in the Emilia-Romagna Region; red with a purple tint, semi-dry and dry, light- to medium-bodied; drink before it is five; serve with lighter foods. Candidate for DOC.

CALABRESE

(kahl-ah-BRAY-suh) Unusual red wine grape grown in the Sicily Region and used in Cerasuolo Di Vittoria (see).

CALABRIA

(kahl-AH-bree-uh) Large Region of 5820 square miles, the "toe of the boot," very mountainous, about 1½ million people; bounded on the N by Basilicata Region, on the E and S by the Ionian and Mediterranean Sea and on the W by the Tyrrhenian Sea; the Capitol city is Reggio Calabria, on the "tip of the toe of the boot." The earliest people were the Bruttii and the Greeks settled there about 800 BC, naming it Brutium; it was conquered by every invader and part of the Kingdom of The Two Sicilies immediately prior to the Risorgimento. The area is known for devastating earthquakes and produces only about 120 million liters of wine annually. See Ciro, Greco di Bianco, Greco di Gerace, Donnici, Pollino, Lamezia, Melissa, etc.

CASTROVILLARI

CIRO

CATANZARO

CALABRIA REGION

GERACE

REGGIO CALABRIA

BIANCO

CALDARO or LAGO DI CALDARO

(kahl-DAHR-oh) KALTERN or KALTERERSEE **DOC** A small town and tiny lake S of Bolzano in Trentino-Alto Adige Region, producing a red wine from 85% Schiava with 15% Pinot Nero/Lagrein grapes; ruby-red to garnet in color, soft, dry, fruity, well-balanced with a slight after-taste of almonds, lighter than the famous Santa Maddelena (see); there is a *classico* zone, a *superiore*, and a *scelto* from selected grapes; best age is under two years; about 25 million liters made annnually.

CALITTO

(kah-LEET-toh) Local wines, both *bianco* and *rosso*, made and consumed on the island of Procida, Bay of Naples, Campania Region; they are light-bodied, good carafe wines.

CALUSO PASSITO and CALUSO PASSITO LIQUOROSO

See Erbaluce.

CAMMELLINO

(kahm-mel-LEEN-oh) A long-necked bottle, about 45″ in overall height, used for Chianti and called a "yard of Chianti" in this country; Florentine in origin, the capacity was formerly one gallon, now 3 + liters. The best Chiantis are bottled in the Bordeaux shape.

CAMPANIA

(kahm-PAHN-ya)   Region of 5250 square miles, 5½ million people, bounded on the N by Lazio and Molise Regions, on the E and S by Puglia and Basilicata Regions, and on the W by the Tyrrhenian Sea. It is famous as the home of Naples (the Capitol city), Mt. Vesuvius, Pompeii and the Isle of Capri in the Bay of Naples. Settled by the Greeks c. 800 BC, conquered by the Romans, the Goths, Byzantine Empire, Normans, and in the 12th Century became part of the Kingdom of Naples. Much of the area is prone to earthquakes — great damage was suffered in November of 1980 — and the average wine production is about 350 million liters...much of it consumed locally; its best-known wines are Capri, Lacrima Christi, Greco di Tufo and Taurasi; there are many more.

1 — Ischia
2 — Procida
3 — Capri

CAMPANIA REGION

CAMPIDANO DI TERRALBA or TERRALBA

(kahm-pee-DAHN-oh dee tair-RAHL-ba)   **DOC**   Either name is correct. Campidano is the large plain N of Cagliari, Terralba a small town, Sardinia the Region; this wine is made from 75% Bovale and 25% Greco/Pascale/Monica and other grapes; it is light ruby-red, dry, medium-bodied, can be 15% alcohol; much rosé is made here but it is not DOC.

CANAIOLO

(kahn-ah-yee-OH-lo)   Excellent red wine grape (a white variety also exists) grown in Tuscany Region; one of the important grapes in Chianti (see).

CANELLI

(kah-NEL-lee)   Small town in Piedmont Region lending its name to a variety of Muscat grape grown there that is much in demand for Asti Spumante.

CANNETTO

(kahn-NAYT-toh)   Red wines made near Casteggio in the Lombardy Region from the Barbera grape plus others; dry, semi-dry and sweet versions are made, as well as a Cannetto Amaro — one of the most popular.

CANNONAU

(kahn-noh-NOW)   Good red wine grape grown all over Sardinia Region, producing many wines in different styles.

CANNONAU DI SARDEGNA

(kahn-noh-NOW dee sar-DAYN-ya)   **DOC**   Excellent red wine from 90% Cannonau grapes made all over Sardinia Region; dark red, tannic when young, 13½% alcohol, aged at least one year before release; a *riserva* with three years age, but drink it before it is six. If it is 15% and two years in wood, it may be a *superiore secco*, *superiore amabile* or *superiore dolce*, depending on the sugar content. There is a fortified classification — *vino liquoroso*, again a *secco* and a *dolce* made. If the grapes are from Oliena, that name may appear on the label. There is a rosé made also.

CANTINA

(kahn-TEE-nah)   A wine cellar; a bar where the public is served.

CANTINA SOCIALE

(kahn-TEE-nah so-CHAH-lay)   An Italian wine firm.

CAPO FERRATO

(KAH-poh fair-RAH-toh)   A tiny point of land E of Cagliari, Sardinia Region, gives its name to this very dark red, dry, tart, strong (15%) wine from the Cannonau grape; too harsh when young, but with age, a well-rounded wine.

CAPO LILIBEO

(KAH-poh lee-lee-BAY-oh)   Good red and white wines named for this point of land near Marsala, Sicily Region.

CAPRI

(KAH-pree) **DOC** A beautiful island in the Bay of Naples, Campania Region, famous as a resort since the days of Rome; home of the famous Blue Grotto (and others). Most unfortunately it is no longer necessary to make the wine from grapes grown on the island itself or to make the wine on the island. This is a ridiculous situation in the opinion of the author.

BIANCO

(bee-AHN-koh) is a light-bodied white wine from Biancolella/Falanghina/Greco grapes, dry and fresh-tasting.

ROSSO

(ROHS-soh) is from Piedirosso grapes and others; ruby-red, light-bodied, dry, carafe wine. Both should be drunk young.

CAPRIANO DEL COLLE

(kah-pree-AHN-oh del KOHL-lay) **DOC** This zone is S of Brescia in the Lombardy Region; production is quite small at this point.

BIANCO

(bee-AHN-koh) is all Trebbiano grapes, straw-colored, dry, fresh, better chilled and to be drunk young.

ROSSO

(ROHS-soh) is made from Sangiovese/Barbera/Merlot grapes; ruby-red, dry, medium-bodied, needs two or three years of age.

CARAFFA

(kah-RAHF-fa) A wine decanter.

CARAMINO

(kahr-ah-MEEN-oh) An excellent dry, full-bodied, red wine from the Novara Hills of Piedmont Region, Nebbiolo and possibly some Bonarda grapes; named for an old castle (pictured on the label) near Fara.

CAREMA

(kah-RAY-ma) **DOC** Superior red wine from the town of Carema in Piedmont Region and the Nebbiolo grape; ruby-red, dry, soft, smooth, full-bodied, aged four years (two in wood) before release, peaks about 6-8 years. One of Piedmont's better wines, it is hard to find as the production is small from the steep, high, hand-worked vineyards — about 125,000 liters made annually; let it breathe upon opening.

CARIGLIANO
(kah-ree-lee-YAH-noh)   Red wine grape grown in the Sicily Region.

CARIGNANO
(kahr-een-YAHN-oh)   Red wine grape grown in Sardinia Region, said to be the same as the Carignane in California.

CARIGNANO DEL SULCIS
(kah-reen-YAH-noh del SOOL-chees)   **DOC**   Sulcis is an ancient name for the island known today as Sant' Antioco off the SW tip of Sardinia (Region); the coastline of this island is overwhelmingly beautiful; there are two wines — *rosato* and *rosso* — the *rosato* is light-bodied, dry and made from the Carignano grapes; the *rosso* is full-bodied, dry, robust — from the same grapes.

CARMIGNANO
(kahr-meen-YAH-noh)   **DOC**   Superior-red wine made from the Chianti grapes (45-65% Sangiovese, 10-20% Canaiolo, 10-20% Trebbiano plus 5% others) and with the important addition of 6-10% Cabernet Sauvignon. Made for 300 years in the town of this name W of Florence in Tuscany Region; dry, full-bodied, well-rounded, but does need age; a *riserva* with three years; generally needs to breathe for several hours. See Vin Ruspo.

CARRICANTE
(kahr-ree-KAHN-tay)   White wine grape grown on the lower slopes of Mt. Etna in Sicily Region; used in Etna wines.

CARTHAGE
(kahr-TAJ-zhay)   Ancient city and city-State founded by Phoenicians *c.* 800 BC on the N coast of Africa near present-day Tunis. The Carthaginians were great explorers, colonists and traders, at one time controlling the western Mediterranean and the W side of Africa as far S as Sierra Leone. It was completely destroyed by Rome at the end of the 3rd Punic War — 146 BC. Every house was destroyed, the site of the city leveled and every survivor sold into slavery. (Those Romans could be rough!)

CARTIZZE
See Prosecco di Conegliano-Valdobbiadene.

CASA VINICOLA
(KAH-sah vee-NEE-koh-lah)   A wine-making firm or a winery as we know it.

CASTEGGIO
(kah-STAYJ-joh)   Small town on the site of the Roman city of Clastidium in Lombardy Region; center of a large grape growing area for Asti Spumante.

CASTEL   or   CASTELLO
A castle.

CASTEL   BRACCIANO
(kahs-TELL-brach-CHAH-no)   Dessert wine made near the town and Lake Bracciano N of Rome, Lazio Region.

CASTEL   CHIURIO
(kahs-TELL kee-OOR-eeoh)   Brand name of two excellent wines made in the Valtellina area of Lombardy Region; the *bianco* is made from Pinot Bianco and Riesling grapes, dry, full-bodied, well-balanced, excellent for aperitifs and lighter meats as well as luncheons; the *rosso* is made from the Nebbiolo grape, dry, full-bodied, but lighter than a Barolo; considered by many to be the best red wine in the Valtellina.

CASTEL   DEL   MONTE
(kahs-TELL del MOHN-tay)   **DOC**   The name means "castle on the mountain" — a fine remnant of the Swabian occupation in the 13th Century — near Bari, Puglia Region; built by Emperor Frederick II as his hunting lodge. The building tends to the Arabic in style and was later used as a prison. This zone is one of the few where different grapes are used in the *rosato* and *rosso*:
BIANCO
(bee-AHN-ko)   is from 65% Pampanuto, 35% Trebbiano/Bombino/Palumbo grapes; straw-colored, dry, fresh, well-balanced, serve chilled and young.
ROSATO
(roh-SAH-toh)   is made from 65% Bombino, 35% Montepulciano/Uva Di Troia grapes, typical rosé color, dry, fruity, drink it young — an excellent rosé.
ROSSO
(ROHS-so)   is from 65% Uva Di Troia, 35% Bombino/Montepulciano/ Sangiovese grapes; ruby-red with an orange tint as it ages (which it needs), dry, varying taste; with three years of age, a *riserva*.

CASTEL   SAN   GIORGIO
(kahs-TELL sahn jee-OR-jee-oh)   Two light but very good wines made in Lazio Region. Candidate for DOC. The *bianco* is from Trebbiano and Malvasia grapes; dry, fruity and fresh; drink it young. The *rosso* is from Sangiovese/Merlot/Montepulciano grapes; ruby-red, dry, needs two to three years of age.

CASTEL   SENURIO
(kahs-TELL say-NOOR-ee-oh)   Brand name for very good red and white wines made in the Sicily Region.

CASTELDACCHIA

(kahs-tel-DACH-cha)   Small town near Palermo, Sicily Region — home of the famous Corvo winery.

CASTELGONDOLFO

Summer home of the Popes in the area S of Rome.

CASTELLER

(kahs-TEL-ler)   **DOC**   Excellent rosé wine made at the N end of Lake Garda, Trentino-Alto Adige Region; typical rosé to light ruby in color, made both dry and semi-dry, from 30% Schiava, 40% Lambrusco, 20% Merlot and 10% other grapes; it does vary in taste.

CASTELLI DI CANELLI

(kahs-TEL-lee dee kah-NEL-lee)   Very good white wine made in the Canelli area, Piedmont Region.

CASTELLI DI IESI (JESI)

See Verdicchio di Castelli di Iesi.

CASTELLI ROMANI

(kahs-TEL-lee roh-MAHN-ee)   aka Colli Romani and Colli Albani — the latter is the DOC name. A geographical term for the area S of Rome — small hills covered with vineyards and crowned with villas, or castles, and tiny villages that have served as a retreat since the days of Rome. A tremendous amount of ordinary carafe wine, *bianco*, *rosato* and some *rosso*, but mostly *bianco*, is produced here — as well as several DOC wines: Colli Albani, Colli Lanuvini, Frascati, Marino, Montecompatri-Colonna and Velletri. The wines have improved greatly in the past two decades; some are still made *amabile* but more apt to be *abboccato*. Drink them young — the younger, the better!

CASTELLO DI GABIANO

(kahs-tel-loh dee gah-bee-AH-no) Excellent red wine from the Barbera grape made in the Monferrato Hills of the Piedmont Region; candidate for DOC. Do not confuse with Castello di Gabbiano, a fine Chianti!

CASTELTAGLIOLO

(kahs-tel-tahl-yee-OH-lo) Important vineyard area producing excellent Cortese grapes in the Piedmont Region.

CASTELVECCHIO

(kahs-tel-VAYK-kee-oh) Brand name for two popular and very good wines made in Sicily Region; the *bianco* is from Catarratto/Grecanico grapes; the *rosso* is from Pignatello/Nerello and other grapes; drink them both young.

CASTIGLIONE FALETTO

(kahs-tee-lee-OH-nay fah-LAYT-to) Excellent red wine from the Nebbiolo grape made in the Piedmont Region.

CATANESE

(kah-tah-NAY-sah) Red wine grape grown in Sicily Region and used in Corvo and other wines.

CATANIA

(kah-TAHN-ya) Important port city of 400,000 on the E coast of Sicily close to Mt. Etna.

CATARRATTO

(kah-tahr-RAHT-toh) Good white wine grape grown in Sicily Region; *catarrato* can be translated "catch the mouse."

CECUBO

(CHAY-koo-boh) Good red wine made S of Aprilia in the Lazio Region since ancient times; from Negroamaro and other grapes; dry, rich and medium-to full-bodied.

CELLARO

(chel-LAHR-oh)   Good red and white wines made in the hills NE of Menfi in Sicily Region.

CELLATICA

(chel-LAH-tee-kah)   **DOC**   Excellent red wine from the hills around the town of Cellatica in the Lake Garda area of Lombardy Region; made from 35-45% Schiava, 25-30% Barbera, 20-30% Marzemino and 10-15% other grapes; ruby-red, medium-bodied, dry, better with a little age, about 500,000 liters produced annually.

CERASUOLO

(chair-ah-soo-OH-loh)   Light red, or cherry-red color; see *Rosato*.

CERASUOLO DI VITTORIA

(chair-ah-soo-OH-loh dee veet-TOHR-ee-ah)   **DOC**   Cerasuolo is the color, Vittoria a city W of Ragusa in Sicily Region; this wine is made from 60% Calabrese, 40% Frappata, to 10% other grapes; dry, full-bodied, strong (16%), harsh when young, but well-balanced with age which it needs; holds for many years.

CERVETERI

(chair-vay-TAIR-ee)   **DOC**   Small town near Civitavecchia, Rome's port, Lazio Region; there are two wines:

BIANCO

(bee-AHN-koh)   is made from 50% Trebbiano, to 30% Verdicchio with the balance of Tocai/Bellone/Bombino grapes; straw-colored, made both *secco* and *amabile*; good carafe wine.

ROSSO

(ROHS-soh)   is made from 25-30% Sangiovese, 25-30% Montepulciano, minimum of 25% Cesanese and the rest a mixture of Canaiolo/Carignano/Barbera; it can be quite good even with this complex allowable formula; dry, ruby-red, with a slightly bitter after-taste.

CESANESE

(chay-sa-NAY-say)   Good red wine grape grown in the Lazio Region, much of it in the area close to Rome; the wine from it is generally medium-bodied, rounded and can be excellent; varies with the producer and the locale.

CESANESE DEL PIGLIO

(chay-sa-NAY-say del PEE-lee-oh) **DOC** Made in and around the town of Piglio about 40 miles SE of Rome, Lazio Region, from 90% Cesanese, 10% Sangiovese/Montepulciano and other grapes; this is a good red carafe wine made *asciutto*, *secco*, *amabile*, *dolce* and a *spumante*. Drink it young.

CESANESE DI AFFILLE or AFFILE

(chay-say-NAY-say dee ahf-FEE-lay) **DOC** The small town of Affile is close to Rome, Lazio Region; the wine is 90% Cesanese, 10% Sangiovese/Montepulciano and other grapes; a good red carafe wine made *asciutto*, *secco*, *amabile*, *dolce* and a *spumante*. Drink it young.

CESANESE DI OLEVANO-ROMANO or
CESANESE DI OLEVANO or CESANESE DI ROMANO

(chay-sa-NAY-sa dee oh-lay-VAH-no / roh-MAHN-oh) **DOC** Made in the same general area SE of Rome, Lazio Region, in these two towns — Olevano and Romano; the grapes are 90% Cesanese, 10% Sangiovese/Montepulciano and others; this red carafe wine is made several ways: *asciutto*, *secco*, *amabile*, *dolce* and a *spumante*; drink it young.

CHAMBAVE

(Fr: shahm-BAHV) A small town in the Aosta Valley and Region known for many years for several superior wines; Vin Rouge de Chambave is made from Barbera/Dolcetto/Grosvein grapes; dry, smooth, full-bodied, better with a little age. Candidate for DOC to include:

Vin Rouge de Chambave,
Vin de Chatillon et St. Vincent (see Chatillon),
Muscat de Chambave. (see Passito di Chambave)

CHARDONNAY

(shar-DOHN-nay) The same superior white wine grape called, incorrectly, Pinot Chardonnay. It is grown to a limited extent in parts of northern Italy and felt by many, over the years, to have been confused with Pinot Bianco!! Never a popular grape in Italy, probably partially because of its low yield, it is being planted in the Trentino-Alto Adige, Fruili-Venezia Giulia, Lombardy and Tuscany Regions. At least one large producer is readying an application for DOC status.

CHATILLON

(Fr: shah-tee-YONH)   A small town in the Aosta Valley and Region producing for years a fine red wine by this name and also as Vin de Chatillon et St. Vincent; the grapes are Petit Rouge/Vien de Nus/Nebbiolo/Dolcetto; they produce a deep red, dry, full-bodied wine. See Chambave.

CHIANTI

(key-AHN-tee)   **DOC**   Undoubtedly the best-known Italian wine throughout the world, more perhaps for the straw-wrapped bottle in the Italian restaurant (a few years ago) than for its finer qualities. There are several stories on the origin of the name; it was also the name of a defensive alliance in the 14th Century — the Chianti League. There are seven areas in the DOC zone:

1) CLASSICO

the area between Florence and Siena, organized in 1924 and using the black rooster (*gallo nero*) on a red-ground-label below the lip of the bottle (silver ground indicates two more years of age and a gold ground three). The wine often needs 4-5 years of age; *vecchio* indicates two years and with three years *riserva* may be used; most producers, however, age their wines much more than the minimum requirement. Contrary to popular opinion in this country, *Classico* does not mean that it is superior to all other Chiantis; some of them may be, but there are many in the other districts that are superior to some *classicos*!

2) COLLI ARETINI

is generally a lighter wine, more acidic; generally to be drunk before it is two years old.

3) COLLI FIORENTINI

from the area S of Florence on either side of the *classico* zone — well-rounded, medium- to full-bodied; often a hint of iris in the bouquet.

4) COLLI SENESI

from the area NW of Siena and also areas SE of that city; similar to Colli Aretini in that it is often lighter and probably should be drunk before it is two years old.

5) COLLINE PISANE

is from the hilly area S of Pisa; some is a little rough or coarse and some is soft and light; frequently slightly *frizzante*.

6) MONTALBANO

a smaller area NW of Florence produces a well-rounded wine, often with a violet aroma.

7) RUFINA

This is an elegant wine with a stronger aroma, well rounded and a longer life. Do not confuse with Ruffino — a brand of Chianti exported to America. The six zones outside the *classico* contain most of the growers who organized their own consortium in 1927 known as the Putto; their trademark is a Bacchus in a Della Robbia wreath, and is a much larger organization than the *Classico* consortium.

There are two types marketed; (1) By far the greater amount is to be drunk young, often bottled in the straw-colored bottle (*fiaschi*), made by the *governo* process, wherein about 10% of lesser grapes are raisined, then crushed and added to the previously-fermented wine, sealed in a vat with a vent for the gas to escape, and left until the following spring when it is bottled. This gives a fresh, slightly effervescent quality to the bottled wine that so many associate with Chianti. A screw-cap is generally used and the contents seldom last beyond three years. The other type (2) is made and aged most carefully, usually bottled in Bordeaux bottles, and, at its best, takes its place among the fine red wines of the world. The grape percentages are the same for all zones: 50-80% Sangiovese, 10-30% Canaiolo, 10-30% Trebbiano/Malvasia and 5% Colorino. The color of Chianti is mostly a deep, deep red with garnet tinges as it ages; it peaks at from 4 to 10 years. The taste is distinctly Chianti — dry, slightly tannic when young, smooth and soft with age. Annual production is about 75-80 million liters.

Prior to DOC legislation there was a large quantity of White Chianti or Chianti Bianco, but that is now prohibited as Chianti is defined as a RED wine. In the last few years there has been agitation to restore that name but without success. However, see Bianco della Lega and Galestro.

CHIANTI AREA IN TUSCANY REGION

1 — CLASSICO
2 — COLLI ARETINI
3 — COLLI FIORENTINI
4 — COLLI SENESI
5 — COLLINE PISANE
6 — MONTALBANO
7 — RUFINA

CHIANTIGIANA

(key-AHN-tee-gee-AHN-ah)   The old road between Florence and Siena, Tuscany Region, going through the Chianti vineyards, now paved and more passable — a delightful way to see the area.

CHIARETTO

(key-ah-RAYT-toh)   means a clear or light wine. The word appears on the Bardolino label of some producers of rosé wines — particularly the lovely Lake Garda rosés. See *Rosato*.

CHIAVENNESCA

(key-ah-vayn-NAS-kah)   The local name in the Valtellina area, Lombardy Region, for the Nebbiolo grape, although the wine it produces here is a little lighter, not as full-bodied and matures quicker than the Piedmont Barolo (its cousin).

CHIERI

(key-AIR-ee)   Small town near Turin in Piedmont Region known for the wine Freisa Di Chieri (see).

CHIETI

(key-AY-tee)   City of 50,000 S of Pescara in the Abruzzo Region; some excellent white wines made here, probably from the Trebbiano and other grapes — much improved in the past 20 years.

CICLOPI

(chee-KLOH-pee)   Brand name for a wine made since the ancient times — today under the Mt. Etna DOC (see).

CILIEGIOLO

(chee-lee-ay-JOH-loh)   Red wine grape grown in Marche, Tuscany and Umbria Regions.

CINQUETERRE

(cheen-kwa-TAIR-rah)   **DOC**   Two very good white wines, hard-to-find, made from 60% Bosco and 40% Albarola/Vermentino grapes in the area N of La Spezia, the SE end of Liguria Region; dry, straw-colored, getting more scarce as the Italian Riviera caters more to the tourist business.

SCIACCHETRA

(shahk-KAY-tra)   A *passito* wine from the same grapes as the table wine above, darker in color, almost amber, 17% alcohol, generally quite sweet. Sciacchetra is translated "chatterer."

CIRO

(CHEE-roh)   **DOC**   A small town just off the coast of the Gulf of Taranto, Calabria Region, and its famous wine — one of the oldest in the world being made today; there is a *classico* zone; about two million liters produced annually and very much improved in the last ten years.

BIANCO

(bee-AHN-koh)   is made from 90% Greco and 10% Trebbiano grapes, straw-colored, light, dry, fruity, best drunk young.

ROSATO

(roh-SAH-toh)   is a pleasant, pinky red light wine from 95% Gaglioppo and 5% Trebbiano/Greco grapes; drink it young.

ROSSO

(ROHS-soh)   is also made from 95% Gaglioppo and 5% Trebbiano/Greco grapes; ruby-red, dry, strong (15% +), full-bodied; it may be a *riserva* with three or more years of age; this is the best of the three and quite long-lived.

CIVITAVECCHIA

(chee-vee-tah-VAYK-kee-ah)   City of 50,000 people in Lazio Region, about 40 miles N of Rome, serving as its port on the Tyrrhenian Sea.

CLASSICO

(KLAHS-see-koh)   Under DOC laws, a smaller portion of a larger area where one wine is produced, and generally considered a superior part of the entire area.

CLASTIDIO

(klahs-TEE-dee-oh)   Brand name for very good wines made in the town of Casteggio, Lombardy Region. The *bianco* is made from Riesling Italico and Riesling Renano grapes, light and semi-dry; the *rosato* is made from Barbera/ Uva Rara/Croatina grapes — dry and a very good flavor; the *rosso* is made from Barbera/Uva Rara/Croatina grapes, quite dry and robust, full-bodied; a *spumante* is made.

CODA DI VOLPE

(KOH-da dee VOHL-pay)   White wine grape grown in Campania Region and used in Greco Di Tufo (see); also a white wine made in Sicily Region.

COLLEPEPE

(KOH-lay-PAY-pah)   Small town in Umbria Region near Todi, producing and consuming very good wines; a *bianco* is made from the Sauvignon and a *rosso* probably from the Sangiovese.

COLLI

(KOHL-lee)   Hills, or a range of hills.

COLLI ALBANI

(KOHL-lee ahl-BAHN-ee)   **DOC**   These hills which surround Lake Albano, about 20 miles S of Rome, Lazio Region, produce a tremendous amount of white wine and have been for thousands of years; they are good carafe wines made from 60% Malvasia Bianco, 25-50% Trebbiano, 15-40% another Malvasia, to 10% Bonvino/Cacchione; the taste will vary with these tolerances, but they are all intended to be drunk young and cool; cellar treatment varies to produce a *secco*, *amabile* and a *spumante*; a *superiore* is available. They have been much improved in the last twenty years.

COLLI ALTOTIBERINI

(KOHL-lee AHL-toh-tee-bair-EE-nee)   **DOC**   This zone is the upper part of the Tiber River valley, N of Perugia, Umbria Region. There are 15 or 20 wines with village names in the area; it remains to be seen if they discontinue those names and adopt the DOC name.

BIANCO
(bee-AHN-koh) is from 70-90% Trebbiano, 10% Malvasia and 20% others; straw-colored, dry, well-balanced wine.

ROSATO
(roh-SAH-toh) is from 50-70% Sangiovese, 10-20% Merlot, other reds to 20% and whites to 10%; dry, fruity and fresh.

ROSSO
(ROHS-soh) from 50-70% Sangiovese, 10-20% Merlot, up to 30% other reds and whites, for a ruby-red, dry, well-balanced wine.

COLLI ARETINI
(KOHL-lee ahr-ay-TEE-nee) One of the seven Chianti zones, (see) producing a slightly more tannic, aromatic Chianti.

COLLI BERICI
(KOHL-lee bear-EE-chee) **DOC** These mountains in the area S of Vicenza in Veneto Region produce excellent wines – all varietally labeled; there are seven:

CABERNET
(kah-bear-NAY) is made from either of the Cabernet grapes or a mixture; ruby-red, dry, robust, typical aroma, needs age – with three years, a *riserva*; peaks about seven.

GARGANEGA
(gar-gah-NAY-ga) is from 90% Garganega and 10% Trebbiano grapes; straw-colored, dry, slightly bitter after-taste.

MERLOT
(mair-LOW) is 100% Merlot grapes; ruby-red, dry, soft, wonderful aroma; drink it before five years of age.

PINOT BIANCO
(PEE-noh bee-AHN-koh) from 85% Pinot Bianco and 15% Pinot Grigio grapes, white-to-yellow, dry, smooth, an excellent wine best drunk young.

SAUVIGNON
(soh-veen-YONH) is 90% Sauvignon and 10% Trebbiano for a straw-colored, dry, full-bodied wine better with a little age.

TOCAI BIANCO
(toh-KIE bee-AHN-Koh) is from 90% Tocai and 10% Garganega grapes; straw-colored, dry, medium-bodied; an excellent aperitif wine best when young and fresh.

TOCAI ROSSO
(toh-KIE ROHS-soh) from 85% Tocai Rosso grapes and 15% Garganega; dry, medium-bodied, tannic when young and needs 2-3 years of age.

COLLI BOLOGNESI or
COLLI BOLOGNESI DI MONTE SAN PIETRO or
COLLI BOLOGNESI DEI CASTELLI MEDIOEVALI
(KOHL-lee boh-loh-NAY-see) **DOC** All names allowed. These hills are SW of Bologna in the Emilia-Romagna Region. Many, if not all, of the wines here are made less dry to go with the richer foods. In addition to the six wines listed, Cabernet Sauvignon is a candidate for DOC.

BARBERA
(bar-BEAR-ah) may be 100% Barbera grape or 15% Sangiovese may be added; deep purple-red, full-bodied, needs age, a *riserva* with three years; peaks about 5 or 6.

BIANCO
(bee-AHN-koh) Good carafe wine made here for hundreds of years; the grapes are 60-80% Albana, 20-40% Trebbiano, made both dry and sweet; also labeled as Bianco Colline Bolognesi from the past.

MERLOT
(mair-LOW) is 85% Merlot with 15% other reds allowed; an excellent wine — ruby-red, dry, soft, also made semi-dry; peaks at 3-5 years.

PINOT BIANCO
(PEE-noh bee-AHN-koh) allows 15% other grapes to be added to the Pinot Bianco; straw-colored, dry and semi-dry; a good carafe wine in its youth!

RIESLING ITALICO
(REES-ling ee-TAHL-ee-koh) 15% other grapes are allowed with the informing grape; there is an opinion that this grape, in this area, is a distinctly native vine called Pignoletto.

SAUVIGNON
(soh-veen-YONH) is 85% Sauvignon grape with 15% other whites allowed; straw-colored, fairly full-bodied, both dry and semi-dry made.

COLLI CIMINI
(KOHL-lee chee-MEE-nee)   Good wines made on the slopes of Mt. Cimini, N of Bracciano, Lazio Region; both *bianco* and *rosso* are made.

COLLI DEL TRASIMENO
(KOHL-lee del trah-see-MAY-noh)   **DOC**   These hills are W of Perugia near Lake Trasimeno in Umbria Region. There are many wines in the area labeled simply "Trasimeno" that are not DOC. Annual production of these two DOC wines is about two million liters:

BIANCO
(bee-AHN-koh) is made from 60-80% Trebbiano and up to 40% Malvasia/Verdicchio/Verdello/Grechetto grapes, for a straw-colored, medium-bodied carafe wine; it can be a little better with age.

ROSSO
(ROHS-soh)   from 60-80% Sangiovese, a maximum of 40% Cigliegiolo/ Gamay/Malvasia/Trebbiano grapes for a garnet-colored, dry, complex wine that is better with a little age.

COLLI DI BOLZANO
(KOHL-lee dee bohl-TZAH-noh)   BOZNER LEITEN   **DOC**   This wine is made near the city of Bolzano in the Trentino-Alto Adige Region; it is from 90% Schiava grapes, red-to-garnet in color, soft and well-balanced, excellent with age.

COLLI DI PARMA
(KOHL-lee dee PAHR-ma)   Except for the E side, this zone surrounds the city of Parma, Emilia-Romagna Region, and is a candidate for DOC. There are several wines:

LAMBRUSCO
(lahm-BROOS-koh)   is a typical wine of this type, from deep rosé to ruby in color, slightly drier than many Lambruscos, aromatic and *frizzante*.

MALVASIA
(mahl-vah-SEE-ah)   A white wine from the Malvasia grape, almost lemon-yellow, smooth, light-bodied and very pleasant.

SAUVIGNON
(soh-veen-YONH)   is from the Sauvignon grape, light gold, dry, good aroma, good grape flavor, excellent wine.

COLLI ETRUSCHI

(KOHL-lee ee-TROO-skee) Hills near Viterbo, Lazio Region, producing red, white and rosé wines — dry and sweet, and a *spumante*.

COLLI EUGANEI

(KOHL-lee oo-GAH-nay-ee) **DOC** These hills are E of Venice and S of Padua, Veneto Region, and like many other areas, have been producing wines for thousands of years.

BIANCO

(bee-AHN-koh) Made from 30-50% Garganega, 20-40% Serprina, 20-30% Tocai/Sauvignon and other grapes, for an excellent dry, smooth, full-bodied wine to be drunk young; a *superiore* is available; also a *spumante*, both sweet and dry.

MOSCATO

(moh-SKAH-toh) is all Moscato Di Canelli grapes; golden, typical Muscat bouquet, sweet, sometimes *frizzante*; a *spumante* is also made.

ROSSO

(ROHS-soh) is made from 60-80% Merlot, 20-40% Cabernet/Barbera/Raboso grapes; dry, ruby-red, soft, a *superiore* and a *spumante* are made. Better with three years of age.

COLLI FIORENTINI

(KOHL-lee fee-or-en-TEE-nee) These hills are outside of Florence to the S and W, producing a fine Chianti (see).

COLLI LANUVINI

KOHL-lee lahn-oo-VEE-nee) **DOC** Also in the Castelli Romani (see) district outside of Rome, Lazio Region, these hills take their name from the town of Lanuvio; this is a white wine made from a maximum of 70% Malvasia, minimum of 30% Trebbiano, and a maximum of 10% Bellone/Bonvino; generally a little more body than others in the area; straw-colored, very pleasant aroma and taste, made both *secco* and *amabile*.

COLLI MORENICI MANTOVANI DEL GARDA

(KOHL-lee mohr-ay-NEE-chee mahn-toh-VAHN-ee del GAHR-da)   **DOC**
The Mantua Hills are S and W of Lake Garda in Lombardy Region; they produce light fresh carafe wines mostly locally consumed and best drunk young!

BIANCO
(bee-AHN-koh) straw-colored, dry, good carafe wine from 20-50% Garganega, 20-25% Trebbiano, 10-40% Pinot Bianco and others.

ROSATO
(roh-SAH-toh) is made from 30-60% Molinara, 20-50% Rondinella and 10-30% Negrara grapes; typical rose color light-bodied, pleasant and dry; a *chiaretto* if 11½%.

ROSSO
(ROHS-so) is made from 30-60% Molinara, 20-50% Rondinella, and 10-30% Negrara grapes; ruby-red, dry, light to medium-bodied, slightly bitter after-taste; may also be labeled *rubino*.

COLLI ORIENTALI DEL FRIULI

(KOHL-lee or-ee-en-TAHL-ee del free-oo-lee)   **DOC**   These hills are N and E of Udine in the Friuli-Venezia Giulia Region and arê often called the Eastern Friuli Hills. The wines made here are all excellent to superior; for many years they were consumed locally or exported to the Northern countries; production has been increasing so we are seeing some of them in this country now. The wines are labeled varietally and must be 95% of that variety.

CABERNET
(kah-bear-NAY) is typical of this grape (either one may be used) ruby-red, dry, smooth, full-bodied; a *riserva* with two years of age and good for five or more.

MERLOT
(mair-LOW) ruby-red, dry, smooth, soft, full-bodied; with two years a *riserva*; peaks at 4-5 years.

PICOLIT
(PEE-koh-leet) is made from *passito* grapes of this variety, sweet, flowery bouquet, deep-yellow, well-balanced, 15% alcohol; a *riserva* with two years of age; very hard to find.

PINOT BIANCO
(PEE-noh bee-AHN-koh) light-yellow to gold, dry, smooth, well-balanced, excellent as an aperitif or with luncheons.

58

PINOT GRIGIO
(PEE-noh GREE-jee-oh)   Almost gold in color, dry, medium-bodied, good as an aperitif and with lighter meats.

PINOT NERO
(PEE-noh NAY-roh)   Ruby-red, dry, characteristic taste, medium-bodied, needs two years of age for a *riserva*; peaks about four.

REFOSCO
(ray-FOHS-ko)   purple-red, dry, full-bodied, slightly bitter after-taste, needs two years of age, but drink it before six. This grape has been grown in this Region for centuries.

RIBOLLA
(ree-BOHL-lah)   This grape produces a light-yellow wine with greenish tints, dry, fresh, strong bouquet.

RIESLING RENANO
(REES-ling ray-NAHN-oh)   Pale yellow in color, dry, smooth, medium-bodied; an excellent wine.

SAUVIGNON
(soh-veen-YONH)   light yellow, dry, smooth and medium-bodied.

TOCAI
(toh-KIE)   Tremendous amount of wine is made from this grape in this Region; it is straw-yellow, dry, smooth and medium-bodied; an above-average carafe wine.

VERDUZZO
(vair-DOOTZ-tzoh)   is yellow to-gold in color; made *secco*, *amabile* and *dolce*, but most of it is *amabile*; there is a lingering fruitiness in this wine; Ramandolo is made from *passito* grapes at this town and is quite sweet.

COLLI PERUGINI
(KOHL-lee pair-oo-JEE-nee)   Hills around the city of Perugia, the Capitol of Umbria Region. Candidate for DOC.

BIANCO
(bee-AHN-koh)   is made from Trebbiano/Malvasia/Grechetto grapes, dry and light-bodied; good as an aperitif wine.

ROSSO
(ROHS-soh)   mostly Sangiovese with some Merlot added and perhaps others; deep red, dry, medium-bodied, excellent wine.

COLLI PESARESI
(KOHL-lee pay-sah-RAY-see)   These hills surround the town of Pesaro in the N end of the Marche Region. See Sangiovese.

COLLI PIACENTINI
(KOHL-lee pee-ah-chen-TEE-nee)   These hills S of the town of Piacenza in the NW corner of Emilia-Romagna Region produce many excellent wines; there is a *bianco* made from Trebbiano that is particularly good; there are two good reds from Barbera and Bonarda. See Gutturnio for DOC wines. See also Ziano.

COLLI ROMANI
See Castelli Romani.

COLLI SENESI

(KOHL-lee say-NAY-see)   One of the seven zones of production of Chianti (see) — the hills outside the city of Siena.

COLLI SPOLETINI

(KOHL-lee spoh-lay-TEE-nee)   Hills outside the city of Spoleto in the S part of Umbria Region, producing good red and white wines from the two basic grapes — Sangiovese and Trebbiano.

COLLI TORTONESI

(KOHL-lee tohr-toh-NAY-see)   **DOC**   These hills surround the city of Tortona in the SE corner of Piedmont Region; two quite different wines are produced — about 1½ million liters.

BARBERA

(bar-BEAR-ah)   From 85-100% Barbera and 15% Bonarda/Dolcetto/Freisa grapes; ruby-red, dry, robust, needs some age; a *superiore* is available.

CORTESE

(kohr-TAY-sah)   from all Cortese grapes, this wine is pale-straw in color, dry, fresh, and has a slight taste of almonds; a *spumante* is made here.

COLLI TUDERTI

(KOHL-lee too-DAIR-tee)   Hills around the city of Todi in SW Umbria Region, producing an excellent white wine, basically a Trebbiano and also a good *rosato* from the Sangiovese, but both must be drunk young!

COLLINE D'AOSTA

(KOHL-leen-ah DAY-ohs-tah)   From the hills around the city of Aosta in that Region; aka Vin de la Colline d'Aoste; a brilliant red wine from Petit Rouge/Pinot Nero/Gamay/Dolcetto grapes; dry, full-bodied, must be aged for one year, usually better with three years. Candidate for DOC under Torrette (see).

COLLINE DE SARRE — CHESALLET

(KOHL-leen-ah duh SAHR SHAY-sah-lay)   Ruby-red, medium-bodied, fresh-tasting wine made from Petit Rouge/Dolcetto/Gamay grapes in the Valle D'Aosta Region. Candidate for DOC under Torrette (see).

COLLINE PISANE

(KOHL-leen-uh pee-SAHN-uh)   Hills S of the city of Pisa, Tuscany Region, making fine Chianti (see) perhaps a little fruitier than some others but does not age as well. There is an excellent white wine made here, basically a Trebbiano, which is a candidate for DOC.

COLLIO GORIZIANO or COLLIO

(KOHL-lee-oh goh-ree-tzee-AH-noh)   **DOC**   Either name is allowed under the DOC regulations. The City of Gorizia (Gorz under the Austrians) is on the border with Yugoslavia and the Friuli-Venezia Giulia Region; these hills are W of that city and have been making wines for 2000 years; they are among the finest produced in this Region. With the exception of Collio, the wines are labeled varietally and are 100% of that variety; there are eleven:

COLLIO
(Kohl-lee-oh)   This white wine is the "quaffing" wine of the area, made all over these hills from 45-55% Ribolla, 20-30% Malvasia and 15-25% Tocai — light, dry, clean and fresh tasting; drink in its first year.

(kah-bear-NAY FRONH)   Ruby-red, medium bodied, pleasantly dry, well-balanced. The Cabernet Sauvignon is not allowed in this zone.

MALVASIA
(mahl-vah-SEE-ah)   is from the variety known as Malvasia Istria and makes a smooth, full-bodied wine, both *secco* and *amabile*.

MERLOT
(mair-LOW)   An excellent red wine, ruby-red, soft, dry, smooth, typical aroma, drink at two and before five. There is much good rosé made here but not DOC.

PINOT BIANCO
(PEE-noh bee-AHN-koh)   Light-yellow with a slight greenish tint, medium-bodied, dry, smooth − an excellent wine.

PINOT GRIGIO
(PEE-noh GREE-jee-oh)   More to the gold in color, dry, full-bodied, smooth. One producer makes a *ramato*, or copper-colored wine from this grape, much richer.

PINOT NERO
(PEE-noh NAY-roh)   Very good red, dry wine from this grape, only medium-bodied, peaks about five years of age.

RIESLING ITALICO
(REES-ling ee-TAHL-ee-koh)   Pale yellow, pleasantly dry, medium-bodied, a good aperitif wine.

SAUVIGNON
(soh-veen-YONH)   Pale-yellow, dry, smooth white wine, a good aperitif or with white meats, from the Sauvignon grape.

TOCAI
(toh-KIE)   Heavily-grown favorite of the Friulians for their every-day white wine – straw-yellow, dry and semi-dry, medium bodied – for "quaffing."
TRAMINER
(trah-MEEN-air)   Deeper-yellow, good spicy taste from this grape we think of as the Gewurztraminer.

COLONNA
See Montecompatri-Colonna.

COLORINO
(KOH-lohr-EE-noh)   Red wine grape grown in Tuscany Region and used in Chianti (see).

COLUMELLA
(koh-loo-MEL-lah)   A Spanish author of a 12-volume treatise on Italian farming, a real classic of husbandry, entitled *De re rustica*, published about 60 AD.

COMO
(KO-moh)   City of 60,000 at the SW end of Lake Como in the Lombardy Region.

CONCA
(KOHN-kah)   Good red wine from Barbera/Canaiolo/Sangiovese/Montepulciano grapes made near Caserta in the N part of Campania Region; dry, full-bodied, better with 2-3 years of age.

CONEGLIANO
(koh-nel-YAH-noh)   Small city of Veneto Region famous for an enological school and excellent white wines – Prosecco di Conegliano (see).

CONSORZIO   –   CONSORTIUM
(kohn-SOHR-tzee-oh)   An association of growers in a specific area, usually organized to conform with the requirements of the ECM (European Common Market).

COPERTINO
(koh-pair-TEE-noh)   **DOC**   A small town in the Salento Peninsula, the "heel of the boot," Puglia Region. There is no *bianco* in the DOC.
ROSATO
(roh-SAH-toh)   made from 70% Negroamaro, 30% maximum of Red Malvasia/Montepulciano/Sangiovese grapes; good rosé color, dry, very pleasant taste.
ROSSO
(ROHS-soh)   also made from 70% Negroamaro and 30% Red Malvasia/Montepulciano/Sangiovese; ruby-red, dry, needs age to soften; slightly bitter after-taste; a *riserva* is available.

CORBERA

(kohr-BEAR-ah) Good white wine from Trebbiano/Inzolia/Catarratto grapes made in Sicily Region — also a rosé and a red wine made here.

CORI

(KOHR-ee) **DOC** Small town about 30 miles SE of Rome, Lazio Region, producing two good wines:

BIANCO

(bee-AHN-koh) from 40-60% Malvasia, 20-30% Bellone and the balance Trebbiano grapes; this straw-colored wine is soft, well-balanced, comes in *secco*, *amabile* and *dolce*.

ROSSO

(ROHS-soh) is good, ruby-red, dry wine from 40-60% Montepulciano, 20-40% Nero Cori and 10-30% Cesanese; needs three to five years of age to be its best.

CORONATA

(kohr-oh-NAH-tah) A famous white wine from Vermentino/Trebbiano/Bianchetta/Rollo grapes; made N of Genoa in Liguria Region since 1600 AD; straw-colored, dry, fresh-tasting, excellent with fish; drink in its first year; hard to find as the production is quite small.

CORTESE

(kohr-TAY-sah) Superior white wine grape grown in Piedmont and Lombardy Regions with a small amount in Sicily Region; it produces an excellent wine, pale straw in color, dry, light-bodied, to be drunk young. *Cortese* means "courteous" in Italian. About ten million liters made annually.

CORTESE DEI COLLI TORTONESI

See Colli Tortonesi

CORTESE DEL RAGUSANO

(kohr-TAY-sah del rah-goo-SAHN-oh) Good white wine made from the Cortese grape near Ragusa in the SE part of Sicily Region.

CORTESE DELL'ALTO MONFERRATO

(kohr-TAY-sah del AHL-toh-mohn-fair-RAH-toh) **DOC** Monferrato is a range of hills near Asti in the Piedmont Region; the grapes are 85% Cortese plus 15% others; the wine is straw-colored, dry, delicate, with a slightly bitter after-taste; made *frizzante* and *spumante*.

63

CORTESE DELL'OLTREPO PAVESE
See Oltrepò Pavese.

CORTESE DI GAVI or GAVI
(kohr-TAY-sah dee GAH-vee) **DOC** Either name is allowed. White wine made in Gavi, a small town in the SE corner of Piedmont Region, from 100% Cortese grapes; straw-colored, dry, fresh and fragrant when young; excellent with fish; a *spumante* is made; this wine has been improved considerably in the last two decades but avoid it if over two years old. About 1½ million liters annual production.

CORVINA
(kohr-VEE-nah) Red wine grape grown in Veneto Region and used in Bardolino and Valpolicella.

CORVO
(KOHR-voh) Proprietary or brand name of a winery in the small town of Casteldacchia near Palermo in Sicily Region, famous throughout the world for many years. The name means "crow" in Italian and refers to an old legend about a hermit, a crow, and a stick to chase the crow; the stick turned into a vine. The term "Prima Goccia" on the label refers to the use of first run juice — in other words, juice from only the first pressing of the grapes. The annual production is about nine million liters.

BIANCO
(bee-AHN-koh) is made from Catarratto and Inzolia grapes, dry, soft, smooth, full-bodied; drink it before it is three years old. A *spumante* is also made.

BIANCO PLATINO
(bee-AHN-koh plah-TEE-noh) is an especially fine dry, light, white wine.

ROSSO
(ROHS-soh) can hold its own with any red meat entree; dry, very well-balanced, full-bodied, made from Perricone and Catanese grapes; drink it before it reaches six.

STRAVECCHIO
(strah-VAY-kee-oh) is a white wine made in the Solera method — deep-gold, dry, strong (16%), and robust.

CORVO ALA
(KOHR-voh AHL-ah) is a *liquoroso* of 16% alcohol, with a flavor of bitter cherries — excellent.

CREME DU VIEN DE NUS
See Vien de Nus and Nus.

CROATINA
(kroh-ah-TEE-nah) Red wine grape in Lombardy Region and said to be the same grape as the Bonarda.

CRU
(KREW) This French word meaning "growth" may not be used on Italian wine labels — ECM ruling. The equivalent word in Italian is *vigneto* (veen-YAY-toh).

D

D.O.C. DENOMINAZIONE DI ORIGINE CONTROLLATA
(day-nom-ee-NAH-tzee-oh-nah dee or-ee-JEEN-ah kohn-trol-LAH-tah)
One can see why it is easier to say "D.O.C."!! This, loosely speaking, is the
group of laws pertaining to and regulating the terms defining the names of
Italian wines. It does not regulate the quality of the wine, but it cannot avoid
contributing to a finer end product. There are five categories of wines,
although the three lowest have not been clearly defined, in the understanding
of the author. From top quality, they are:

      1) **D.O.C.G.**   2) **D.O.C.**   3) **Vini tipici**
    4) **Vini da tavola con indicazione geografica**   5) **Vini da tavola.**

DOCG category. These wines not only meet the requirements for the DOC
wines (below) but are guaranteed by the Italian government to be as
labeled. The "G" stands for "*guarantita*" or guaranteed. The details
involved have apparently delayed elevating very many wines to this
rank. Mentioned for this exalted status are: Barolo, Barbaresco,
Brunello Di Montalcino, Vino Nobile Di Montepulciano, Chianti,
Albana Di Romagna and Vernaccia Di San Gimignano.

DOC category. The number of wines, or zones, in this category stands
at over 200 depending on how they are counted, and may increase to
approximately 250 which will involve under 20% of the total production. They are listed in the Appendix under their Regions. The term
"zone" seems more appropriate since there are from one to seventeen
wines in each area, or zone. The type of soil is defined, the types of
grapes grown and the quantities produced − all are regulated, and
recorded for inspection purposes; in short, DOC on the label amounts
to a pedigree. Quality is not regulated but it cannot help but improve
under this system. One important point is that if a grower produces
more wine than allowed or a sample of his wine is below standard, his
entire production for that year is denied DOC status! This is more
stringent regulation than in other countries − and all for
the best!!

NOTE: In the original law passed in 1963 there was a category named
D.O.S. The "S" is for *semplice*, Italian for simple or plain. That
category has been eliminated in favor of the following:

VINI TIPICI This category has not been used on wine labels, if indeed it has been organized by the government. Since *"tipici"* is translated "typical," it will have to be defined carefully.

VINI DA TAVOLA CON INDICAZIONE GEOGRAFICA This category is not yet in widespread use. It will probably be limited in the beginning to naming the area and the varieties of grapes in the wine.

VINI DA TAVOLA Here we have a phrase that has been used on wine labels in Italy for many, many years; and also on wines made in America by Italians! Wordwise, it simply means "table wine" and, as such, could include everything made! It will include wines that do not meet DOC requirements on varieties and quantities; it will probably include all brand names; as such then, the reputation of the vintner or shipper will be all-important. Take for example, Sassicaia, which topped all Cabernet wines in a world-tasting in London — this wine would be labeled *Vino Da Tavola*!! It will not conform to any DOC! The same, then, will also be true of Corvo, Fiorano, Pomino, Sogno Di Baco, Tignanello and many others which are far superior to many DOC wines!! The task confronting those responsible is not an easy one.

DAMASCHINO
(dah-mah-SKEE-noh) White wine grape grown in the Sicily Region and the wine made from it.

DE, DEI, DEL, DELLA, DI
Various forms meaning, very loosely, "of."

DEL MAGNIFICO
(del mag-NEE-fee-koh) Brand name for red and white wines highly advertised and sold in this country.

DEPOSITATA
(day-poh-see-TAH-ta) Registered.

DIOCLETIAN
(dee-oh-KLAY-shun) was a Roman Emperor who passed the first laws fixing the prices of wines — in 301 AD.

DISCIPLINARI
(dee-see-plee-NAHR-ee) The "discipline" or details defining all phases of growing, production, etc., for the finished wine to qualify for DOC status.

DOLCE
(DOHL-chay) Very sweet. The progression:

secco — to 1% sugar; *abboccato* — 1-2½% sugar;
amabile — 2½-3% sugar; *dolce* — from 3-6% sugar.

DOLCEAQUA
See Rossese Di Dolceaqua.

DOLCETTO

(dohl-CHAYT-toh) Very good red wine grape — the grape is sweet — and the wine from it, dry, soft, soon-ready and well-balanced; best drunk young as its best qualities have been developed by the time it is two years old; avoid it if over five. There are about 2½ million liters produced annually. DOC requires the town of origin be named; all these are in the Piedmont Region:

DOLCETTO D'ACQUI

(dohl-CHAYT-toh DAH-kee) **DOC** This wine comes from S of Asti and Alessandria; if aged for one year, a *superiore*. See Dolcetto above.

DOLCETTO D'ALBA

(dohl-CHAYT-toh DAHL-bah) **DOC** Made in and around the town of Alba; supposedly the best from this grape; a *superiore* with one year of age. See Dolcetto above.

DOLCETTO D'ASTI

(dohl-CHAYT-toh DAS-tee) **DOC** The grapes must be from this area; a *superiore* with one year. See Dolcetto above.

DOLCETTO D'OVADA

(dohl-CHAYT-toh doh-VAH-da) **DOC** This town is S of Asti and the grapes must come from it; this wine is generally a little sweeter than the others; a *superiore* is available. See Dolcetto above.

DOLCETTO DELLE LANGHE MONREGALESI

(dohl-CHAYT-toh del-luh mohn-ray-GAHL-ay-see) **DOC** These grapes must come from the sides of the Langhe Hills; a *superiore* is available. See Dolcetto above.

DOLCETTO DI DIANO D'ALBA

(dohl-CHAYT-toh dee dee-AHN-oh DAHL-ba) **DOC** Diano is a small village S of Alba; a *superiore* is made. This wine is second only to that from Alba (above).

DOLCETTO DI DOGLIANI

(dohl-CHAYT-toh dee doh-glee-AHN-ee) **DOC** Dogliani is a small town producing these grapes; a *superiore* is available. See Dolcetto above.

DON ALFONZO

(DOHN ahl-FOHN-tzoh) Brand name for local *bianco*, *rosato* and *rosso* wines made and consumed on Ischia island in the Bay of Naples, Campania Region; included here for nostalgic Americans!

DONNAZ

(dohn-NAHTZ) **DOC** A superior red wine from 85% Nebbiolo grapes, grown high in the mountainous Valle D'Aosta Region. Donnaz is the name of a small town in this French-speaking area where the Nebbiolo grape is known as the Picoutener (Fr: PEE-koo-ten-ay); the wine is bright red, medium- to full-bodied, dry, very nice after-taste, must be aged for three years (two in wood) before release, and will age for many more; it may peak about five in the lesser vintages. The area has made this wine for over 1000 years!

DONNICI

(DOHN-nee-chee) **DOC** A small town S of Cosenza in the Calabria Region is the source of this name and its wine; there is no *bianco* in the DOC; most of the annual production of 100,000 liters is drunk locally.

ROSATO

(roh-SAH-toh) is made of 50% Gaglioppo, 10-20% Greco Nero, a minimum of 20% Malvasia/Mantonico/Pecorella grapes; typical rosé in color, light and dry; drink in its first year.

ROSSO

(ROHS-soh) is also from 50% Gaglioppo, 10-20% Greco Nero, a minimum of 20% Malvasia/Mantonico/Pecorella grapes; dry, medium-bodied, and peaks about five years.

DONZELLE

(dohn-TZAY-la) Two very good wines, *bianco* and *rosso*, made in Sicily Region under this brand name; "*donzelle*" is translated "damsel" or "country girl."

DORATO DI SORSO

(doh-RAH-toh dee SOHR-soh) A small town in Sardinia Region makes this very good aperitif wine from the Cannonau grape; white-to-pink, dry and strong (15%).

DORGALI

(dohr-GAHL-ee)   A small town W of Nuoro, Sardinia Region, producing an excellent *rosato* and *rosso* from Cannonau grapes; the *rosato* is dry and full of flavor; the *rosso* is dark ruby-red, dry and robust, 15%, also made in *amabile* style.

DRACENO

(drah-CHAY-noh)   A brand name for very good *bianco*, *rosato* and *rosso* wines made NW of Menfi in the SW part of Sicily Region.

DREPANO

(dray-PAH-noh)   A brand name for good wines made in the very western tip of Sicily Region; the *bianco* is from Catarrato and Grillo grapes, dry, fresh-tasting and pleasant; the *rosato* is made from Perricone and Grillo grapes, dry, good rosé color, light in body; the *rosso* changes grapes to Nero d'Avola and Nerello — for a bright red, medium-bodied, dry wine.

DURELLO

(doo-REL-loh)   White wine grape not widely grown, but producing a very good wine — in Veneto Region; pale-straw in color, light, dry, and fruity; often *frizzante* but generally made as *spumante*.

E

EASTERN FRIULI HILLS
— a hilly area N and E of the city of Udine in the Friuli-Venezia Giulia Region; for wines of the area, see Colli Orientali del Friuli.

ELBA
(ELL-ba) **DOC** A small island 5 miles or so off the coast of Tuscany and part of that Region; more famous as the exiled home of Napoleon than for its wines; there are beautiful mountains, beaches and coast line — and almost 700,000 liters of wine made here annually. There is no *rosato* in the DOC.

BIANCO
(bee-AHN-koh) is from 90% Trebbiano grapes, light-yellow, dry, good carafe wine; best when young; a good *spumante* made here — fairly dry.

ROSSO
(ROHS-soh) must be 75% Sangiovese with a maximum of 25% Canaiolo/ Trebbiano/Biancame grapes; deep red, medium-bodied, needs age; a *spumante* is also made.

ELORO
(AY-lohr-oh) Brand name for good red and white wines made S of Syracuse in Sicily Region; mostly consumed locally; the *bianco* is made from Catarratto/Inzolia/Albanello grapes, straw-colored, dry, light, better with a little age; the *rosso* is made primarily from the Calabrese, dry, full-bodied, strong (16%), needs two or three years of age.

EMILIA — ROMAGNA

(ay-MEE-le-ya roh-MAHN-ya)   A large Region of 8,542 square miles in the north central part of Italy, bordered on the N by Lombardy and Veneto Regions, on the E by the Adriatic Sea, on the S by Marche and Tuscany Regions, and on the W by Liguria, Piedmont and Lombardy Regions; There are over four million population and the Capitol city of Bologna has often been called "The Gourmet Capitol of the World." After the Fall of Rome it was conquered by the Lombards, Byzantine Empire and the Franks among others; parts of it were in the Duchy of Modena, the Duchy of Parma and the Papal States until the Risorgimento of the 1860s. The average annual wine production is close to one billion liters! It is also famous for its very rich cooking, Parmesan cheese, fruit orchards and, of course, Lambrusco, as well as many fine DOC wines.

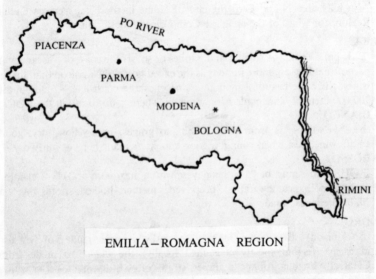

EMILIA — ROMAGNA   REGION

ENFER D'ARVIERS

(Fr: AHN-fair DAR-vey-ay)   **DOC**   Excellent red wine from the Petit Rouge grape (85%) near the town of Arviers in the Valle D'Aosta Region. "Enfer" is translated as "inferno" from the very hot summer sun in the immediate area. The wine is dry, rich, full of flavor, best with more age than the one year required; some tasters find a flavor of Alpine flowers.

ENOTECA

(ay-noh-TAY-ka)   A collection or display of wines for a given area — whatever limits may be chosen. Many have been started in Italy in the last ten years — both publicly and privately financed. The Italian Wine Promotion Center at 499 Park Avenue in New York City encompasses one displaying over 2000 wines from all over Italy.

ENOTRIA

(ay-NOH-tree-ah)   Loosely — "land of wine."

EPOMEO

(ay-poh-MAY-oh)   (1)   Extinct volcano on the island of Ischia, Bay of Naples, Campania Region, which last erupted in the 14th Century. (2)   Red and white wines made and consumed there — light, dry and semidry, good carafe wines.

ERBALUCE

(air-bah-LOO-chay)   Good white wine grape grown in the N part pf Piedmont Region.

ERBALUCE DI CALUSO

(air-bah-LOO-chay dee kah-LOO-soh)   **DOC**   This excellent white wine is made from the Erbaluce grape in the town of Caluso N of Turin in Piedmont Region; straw-colored, dry, fresh-tasting, best in its youth — under two years. Annual production is over one million liters.

CALUSO PASSITO

(koh-LOO-soh pahs-SEE-toh)   **DOC**   This wine is 95% Erbaluce and 5% Bonarda grapes, allowed to "raisin" or *passito*; gold-to-amber, sweet, fullbodied, smooth and strong (14%) and must be aged five years; drink it soon after.

CALUSO PASSITO LIQUOROSO

(kah-LOO-soh pahs-SEE-toh lee-kor-OH-so) **DOC** Made from the *passito* wine above, then fortified; it is similar in taste, at least 16% alcohol and aged for five years.

ERICINO

(air-ee-CHEE-no)   Good wines from the village of Erice near Trapani at the W end of Sicily Region; the *bianco* is made from Catarrato/Inzolia/Grillo/ Trebbiano grapes; pale-straw in color, dry and light; the *rosso* is made from an unusual mixture — Barbera/Trebbiano/Vernaccia grapes — and is deep red, slightly fruity, dry and soft.

EST! EST!! EST!!!

DOC   In 1110 AD, a Monsignor Hans Fugger (another version makes him a Bishop) on his way to (or from) Rome, is supposed to have drunk himself to death on the wine in Montefiascone — or so says the statement on his tomb in the church of St. Flavian. His man-servant was to scout the inns ahead of his master and mark those suitable with an "Est" on the outside wall; he apparently was over-enthusiastic about this one! For many years a barrel of the local wine was poured on the prelate's tomb on the anniversary of his death. The wine made there today is from 65% Trebbiano, 20% Malvasia and 15% Rossetto grapes; light- to medium-bodied, made both *secco* and *abboccato* — a pleasant wine for luncheon when served cool and young. The town of Montefiascone is about 50 miles N of Rome, near Lake Bolsena, in the Lazio Region.

ETICHETTA

(ay-tee-KAYT-ta)   The label on the bottle.

ETNA

(ETT-na)   **DOC**   Wines made around this active volcano on the E side of Sicily Region; the first-known eruption of this 10,700 foot volcano was in 475 BC, the last major eruption in 1950-51, minor ones in 1977, 1979 and 1981. Vines grown on the lower slopes produce about 1¼ million liters of wine annually.

BIANCO

(bee-AHN-ko)   From 60% Carricante, to 40% Catarrato and 15% Trebbiano grapes; straw-colored, light-bodied, dry, fresh-tasting wine. Drink it young.

BIANCO SUPERIORE

(bee-AHN-ko soo-pay-ree-OHR-ay)   is made but must have at least 80% Carricante grapes, is from Milo and was formerly labeled Bianco Di Milo.

ROSATO

(roh-SAH-toh)   is a typical rosé wine made from at least 80% Nerello grapes, dry, medium-bodied; drink it young.

ROSSO

(ROHS-soh)   is also from 80% Nerello grapes, ruby-red, dry, medium-bodied, well-balanced, better with a little age — three or so years.

ETRURIA — ETRUSCANS

The ancient name for parts of Tuscany, Lazio and Emilia-Romagna Regions, and the home of this ancient people thought to have come from Asia Minor as early as 1200 BC. Their alphabet has so far defied all efforts to translate. Their main area was from the Po River to Rome, although late finds have placed them as far north as the Isarco River valley and as far south as the Puglia Region. They were extremely intelligent with the highest degree of civilization known prior to the Roman Empire; were also wealthy and possessed extensive knowledge of iron-working and bronze. They are also credited with introducing irrigation to Italy, inventing the chariot (previously credited to the Romans) before being conquered by them about 500 BC. Pottery, bronzes and their gold work spread as far as France and Germany.

EUGANEAN HILLS

are in Veneto Region; for wines see Colli Euganei.

F

FALERIO DEI COLLI ASCOLANI
(fah-LAY-ree-oh-day KOHL-lee ahs-koh-LAHN-ee) **DOC** This wine was known for years simply as Falerio Bianco. It comes from the hills in the SE corner of the Marche Region; the grapes are 75-80% Trebbiano with the balance of Passerina/Verdicchio/Malvasia/Pinot Bianco/Pecorino; straw-colored, light-bodied and dry; to be drunk young.

FALERNO — FALERNUM
(fah-LAIR-no — fah-LAIR-num) Wines have been produced in this area — halfway between Rome and Naples — since the days of Rome and are still grown today under the same name.

FALERNO
is a **ROSSO** made from Aglianico and other grapes, dry, pleasant aroma; better with a little age but drink it before its fifth birthday.

FALERNO BIANCO
(fah-LAIR-noh bee-AHN-koh) or FALERNUM is from the Falanghina and other grapes, straw-colored, dry, strong, best chilled and drunk young.

FARA
(FAHR-ah) **DOC** An excellent red wine named for this town in the Novara Hills, Piedmont Region; made from 30-50% Nebbiolo, 10-30% Vespolina and to 40% Bonarda grapes; it is ruby-red, dry, full-bodied, and must be aged for three years (two in wood) before release; better with a few more years; about 50,000 liters made annually.

FARO

(FAHR-oh)　**DOC**　Faro is translated "lighthouse" — one of Sicily's best red wines; it comes from near Messina in the NE corner of Sicily Region and is from 60-90% Nerello, 5-10% Nocera, and to 15% Calabrese/Gaglioppo/Sangiovese grapes; red, dry, full-bodied, needs to age five years to be smooth; the production is limited and the wine, although hard to find, is worth it! Serve with red meats.

FAUSTUS

(FOW-stoos)　Brand name for red, white and rosé wines made near Palermo in Sicily Region.

FENICIO

(fay-NEE-chee-oh)　A white wine from Grillo grapes from the island of Mothia off Marsala, the W end of Sicily Region; amber in color, dry, medium-bodied.

FIANO

(fee-AHN-oh)　Good white wine grape grown on Capri and the mainland of Campania Region.

FIANO DI AVELLINO

(fee-AHN-oh dee AH-vel-LEE-no)　**DOC**　Named for the small town of Avellino about 30 miles due E of Naples, Campania Region, this wine is from the Fiano grape, dry, smooth, delicious flavor, fruity, an excellent white wine best served chilled. The area sustained heavy damage in the 1980 earthquake.

FIASCO

(fee-AHS-koh)　Flask; formerly used heavily for Chianti.

FIORANO

(fee-oh-RAH-noh)　Brand name for superior wines made S of Rome in the Lazio Region. An example of superb wines that may legally use only the phrase "Vino da Tavola." The *bianco* uses different grapes but it is a superior white wine from all standards; there is a touch of Malvasia but yet it is dry. The *rosso* is made from equal parts of Cabernet Sauvignon and Merlot grapes; a superior red wine, dry, full-bodied, rich, smooth and velvety; aged at least two years in wood and better with a few more years. Available in limited quantity as the production is still quite small.

Vino da Tavola
FIORANO

FIANO DI AVELLINO

FIRENZE

(fee-REN-tzay)   Italian for the city we call Florence; it is the Capitol of the Tuscany Region, 500,000 population; bisected by the Arno River. It served as the Capitol of Italy from 1865 until the seizure of Rome in 1870. This, the Golden City of the Renaissance, was controlled by the Medici family for almost two centuries and is filled with magnificent art treasures, museums, palaces, gardens, libraries; the Uffizi Gallery has one of the most important art collections in the world; its mundane aspect is as the center of today's Chianti trade!

FLUFUNS

Etruscan god of wine (contemporary of Bacchus?).

FOGGIA

(FOHJ-jah)   City of 75,000 population in the N part of Puglia Region, site of a beautiful cathedral and center of wine trade today.

FORASTERA

(for-ah-STAIR-ah)   White wine grape grown on the island of Ischia, Campania Region, and used in Ischia Bianco; also the name of a wine made there — straw-colored, dry, fresh-tasting; sometimes *frizzante*.

FORMIA

(FOHR-mee-ah)   Town N of Naples, Campania Region, Source of the ancient wines Falernia and Formican; the area is heavily planted with vines today but the wines made are not among Italy's best.

FRACIA

(FRAH-cha)   Brand name for an excellent red wine from the Nebbiolo grape made near Sondrio — the Valtellina area of Lombardy Region; see Valtellina Superiore for more information.

FRANCIACORTA

(FRAHN-chee-ah-KOR-ta)   **DOC**   Odd name for two wines made near the town of Cortefranca, near Brescia, Lombardy Region; note that PINOT is used instead of BIANCO. Production is about one million liters annually.
PINOT
(PEE-noh)   Made from the Pinot Bianco grape, pale yellow with slight greenish tint, soft, fresh-tasting, excellent fish wine; drink it young; a *spumante* is made which allows Pinot Grigio and Pinot Noir grapes, some made by *metodo champenois*.
ROSSO
(ROHS-soh)   Made from 40-50% Cabernet Franc, 20-30% Barbera, 15-25% Nebbiolo and 10-15% Merlot — a most unusual combination of grapes that gives an excellent dry, full-bodied, well-rounded wine with a little age; let it breathe for an hour.

FRAPPATA

(FRAHP-pah-ta)   Good white wine grape grown in the Sicily Region, used in many of their wines.

FRASCATI

(frah-SKAH-tee) **DOC** Another of Italy's well-known wines, made around the town of Frascati in the Alban Hills S of Rome, Lazio Region, one of the best of the Castelli Romani wines; the grapes are 90% of various Malvasias and Greco with a maximum 10% of Bellone/Bombino; always a smooth wine, well-rounded, delightful aroma, best drunk young; it is made several ways: *secco*, *amabile*, *dolce* which may be called *Cannellino*; a *superiore* is available and a *spumante*.

FRECCIAROSO

(fray-cha-ROHS-soh) A brand name for excellent wines popular in Lombardy Region as well as here; the name is translated "red arrow" and they are made in Casteggio, Lombardy Region. Those wonderful brand names La Vigne Blanche, Sillery, St. George and Grand Cru can no longer be used as the wines now made conform to the DOC regulations for the Oltrepò Pavese zone.

FREISA

(FRAY-sa) Superior red wine grape grown primarily in Piedmont Region, and the wine made from it — sometimes sweet, *frizzante*, often better with a little age; a *spumante* made. About 30 million liters produced annually.

FREISA D'ASTI

(FRAY-sa DAH-stee) **DOC** Excellent red wine from the Freisa grape grown on the Monferrato hillsides in Piedmont Region; purple-red with orange tints as it develops, slight flavor of raspberry; made *secco*, *amabile* with a *superiore* available; also a *frizzante naturale* and a *spumante naturale*. Probably at its best by the end of the second year.

FREISA DELLE LANGHE

(FRAY-sa del-la LAHN-gay) A good red wine from the Freisa grape and the Langhe Hills in Piedmont Region; a *spumante* made here; see above entries; drink before it is five.

FREISA DI CHIERI

(FRAY-sa dee kee-AIR-ee) **DOC** Excellent red wine from the Freisa grape and the town of Chieri, SE of Turin, Piedmont Region; it is considered to be the best of the wines from this grape; a beautiful ruby-red, smooth and well-rounded; both *secco* and *amabile* made; also a *frizzante* and a *spumante*; a *superiore* is available. Drink it before it is five.

FRIULI — VENEZIA GIULIA

(free-OO-lee veh-NAY-tzee-ah JOO-lee-ah)   A Region of 2948 square miles, 1½ million people, Capitol city is Udine; it is the NE corner of Italy, bordered on the N by Austria, on the E by Yugoslavia, on the S by the Adriatic and on the W by Veneto Region. After the Roman Era, it was invaded many times and almost destroyed by some of the more vicious conquerors; part of Venetia about 1000AD, and under Austrian control until after World War I; the vineyards were gutted in WWII, but are bearing heavily once again. This Region is different in its handling of DOC wines — there are six zones: Grave Del Friuli, Colli Orientali, Aquileia, Isonzo, Latisana and Collio Goriziana, each including a number of different wines instead of the usual zone where only one or two wines are made. A very serious earthquake damaged much of the area N of Udine in 1976. The average annual wine production is over 125 million liters.

FRIZZANTE

(free-ZAHN-tay)   Slightly sparkling, but not artifically carbonated.

FUSTINO

(foo-STEEN-no)   Small wine barrel, decanter-sized.

FRIULI – VENEZIA REGION

G

GAGLIOPPO

(gahl-ee-OHP-poh)   Good red wine grape grown in Calabria Region (Ciro) and in Sicily Region (Faro).

GALESTRO

(gahl-AY-stroh)   For several years, producers in the Chianti area have sought an outlet for the over-abundance of white grapes, as White Chianti or Chianti Bianco, was prohibited by DOC — (Chianti was decreed to be a red wine). Several large producers in the Chianti Putto consortium developed Galestro, a white wine made from Trebbiano (mostly), Sauvignon, Chardonnay and Pinot Bianco — a dry, light, fresh, fruity wine that is a candidate for DOC. The production in 1980 was about three million liters. See also Bianco Della Lega.

GAMAY

(gah-MAY)   The same red wine grape from the Beaujolais area of France is grown in limited areas in Italy; a good red wine is made from it in the Colli Bolognesi in the Emilia-Romagna Region; it is also used in some local wines in Umbria and the Valle D'Aosta Regions; there is little, if any, resemblance to the wine produced in France.

GAMBELLARA

(gam-bel-LAHR-ah) **DOC** Very good white wine from the town of Gambellara near Soave in the Veneto Region; made from 80-90% Garganega and 10-20% Trebbiano grapes, dry, well-balanced, best when young; a *superiore* is available. See Recioto Di Gambellara and Vin Santo Di Gambellara.

GARDA

See Lago Di Garda.

GARGANEGA

(gahr-GAHN -ay-ga) Superior white wine grape grown in Veneto Region, used in Soave and Gambellara wines, among others.

GARIBALDI, GIUSEPPE

(joo-SEP-pee gahr-ee-BAHL-dee) 1807-1882. Early patriot born in Nice when it was part of Savoy (Piedmont); perhaps more responsible for leading the Unification of Italy than any other one person.

GATTINARA

(gaht-tee-NAHR-ah) **DOC** Superior and famous red wine named for the town of Gattinara and made there for over 1000 years; from 90% Nebbiolo grapes called the Spanna in this area (and often so labeled) and with 10% Bonarda allowed; one of Italy's finest red wines — round, smooth, full-bodied, great flavor and long life; must be aged four years (two in wood) before release. About 400,000 liters produced annually. Best age — from 8 to 12 years, although the best vintages produce a magnificent wine capable of much longer life.

GAVI or CORTESE DI GAVI

(GAH-vee) **DOC** Either name is allowed. White wine made in the small town of Gavi in the SE corner of Piedmont Region, from 100% Cortese grapes; straw-colored, dry, fresh and fragrant when young; excellent with fish; a *spumante* is made; while this wine has improved tremendously in the past two decades, avoid it if over two years old. About 1½ million liters produced annually.

GENOVA

(JAY-noh-va)   We call it Genoa! Italy's largest port and a beautiful city of 700,000 people; the Capitol of Liguria Region; famous in history; many Medieval churches and palaces; one of the foremost City-States and Maritime Republics, great naval history, etc., etc. An important stop on the tourist run.

GENZANO

(jen-TZAH-no)   A small town in the Castelli Romani area of Lazio Region, producing much good wine.

GERACE

(jay-RAH-chay)   Small town in Calabria Region famous for its wine — Greco Di Gerace (see).

GEWURTZTRAMINER

This superior white wine grape is known in Italy as the Traminer Aromatico or sometimes just as Traminer. Its home supposedly is the village of Tramino, in the Trentino-Alto Adige Region.

GHEMME

(GAYM-may)   **DOC**   A small town in the Piedmont Region and the wine made there since the 13th Century; from 60-80% Nebbiolo, 10-30% Vespolina and up to 15% Bonarda, this excellent red has a bouquet of violets, a garnet color, is dry, smooth and full-bodied; it must have four years of age (three in wood) before release and will live for many more, especially from the better years; annual production approaches 150,000 liters.

GIGLIANO

(jee-lee-AH-no)   A very good rosé wine made in the Puglia Region from Malvasia and Negroamaro grapes.

GIRO

(JEE-roh)   Red wine grape grown in Sardinia Region, believed to have been brought from Spain.

GIRO DI CAGLIARI

(JEE-roh dee KAHL-yar-ee) **DOC** Good red wine, strong (15%), rich, full-bodied, well-balanced, from the Giro grape near Cagliari on the S coast of Sardinia Region; made in two ways — *secco* and *dolce naturale*, good for five years; two fortified styles — *liquoroso secco naturale* and *liquoroso dolce naturale*; there is a *riserva* in the fortified wines. Annual production less than 15,000 liters.

GORIZIA — GORIZIA HILLS

(gor-EE-tzee-ah) A city of 40,000 people on the Isonzo River bordering Yugoslavia; known as Gorz under the Austrian occupation; the hills are W of the city; see Collio Goriziana for wines; the Region is Friuli-Venezia Giulia.

GOVERNO

(goh-VAIR-noh) A process whereby a small amount of slightly raisined grapes (*passito*) are added to an already-fermented wine — sealing both in one vat with a vent for the gas to escape, for several months — the end result being a prickly taste. This method has been used in inexpensive Chianti and Valpolicella (and perhaps others) and is said to preclude wines so made from aging — although this, too, is debated.

GRAGNANO

(grahn-YAH-no) Very good red wine from the town of Gragnano between Naples and Sorrento, Campania Region; from the Aglianico and Piedirosso grapes, dry and semi-dry, medium-bodied; sometimes a hint of strawberries in the taste.

GRAN CARUSO

(GRAHN-kah-ROO-soh) Proprietary or brand name for very good red, white and rosé wines served at a famous inn at Ravello; included here for nostalgic Americans!

GRAUVERNATSCH

German name for a good, strong, dry, red wine from the Schiava grape, made near the town of Terlano in the Trentino-Alto Adige Region.

GRAVE DEL FRIULI

(GRAH-vay del free-OO-lee) **DOC** This zone is really an extension of the Eastern Friuli Hills N and E of Udine in the Friuli-Venezia Giulia Region; the change in name is from the change in soil — to a gravel from the hill soil — ("grave" is gravel). For a long time, production was not great enough to export much wine, but recent increases allow much more to be exported. There is a large amount of rosé here, much of it from the Merlot grape and a lot of *spumante* from the Moscato grape — neither are DOC at this time. Each wine is labeled with the grape variety and must be 90% of that variety.

CABERNET

(kah-bear-NAY) may be from the Cabernet Franc or the Cabernet Sauvignon grape, or a mixture; ruby-red, excellent Cabernet flavor, softer than many wines from this grape, although it can be quite full-bodied requiring medium age; it is dry and needs to breathe for at least an hour; good with roast beef; best age 5 to 10 years.

MERLOT

(mair-LOW)   The Merlot grape makes an excellent, even superior, red wine here — dry, soft, ready to drink — a wine for red meat; drink before its fifth birthday.

PINOT BIANCO

(PEE-no bee-AHN-koh)   The Pinot Bianco grape makes a pale-yellow-to-gold, dry, soft wine with a slight almond taste, good as an aperitif and with fish and chicken, best drunk young. A *spumante* is made, but not DOC.

PINOT GRIGIO

(PEE-noh GREE-jee-oh)   This grape makes a golden yellow wine, characteristically light and dry. Good as an aperitif, with soups, roast pork; best chilled and young.

REFOSCO

(ray-FOHS-ko)   This grape makes a wine that is a deep purple-red, dry, with a slightly bitter after-taste, good with a full-flavored meat entree.

TOCAI

(toh-KIE)   labeled as Tocai or Tocai Friulano; light-yellow, dry, well-balanced, good as an aperitif, with fish and chicken; best drunk young.

VERDUZZO

(vair-DOOTZ-tzoh)   is a golden color, medium dry or dry, full-bodied, slightly bitter after-taste; serve chilled.

GRECANICO

(gray-KAHN-ee-koh)   White wine grape grown in Sicily Region and the wine made from it.

GRECHETTO

(gray-KET-toh)   Good white wine grape grown in central Italy; used in Orvieto, Torgiano and other wines.

GRECO

(GRAY-koh)   Superior white wine grape thought to have been brought from Greece when they were colonizing the central and southern part of the Peninsula; grown and used in wines in Umbria, Lazio, Calabria and Campania Regions.

GRECO DI BIANCO

(GRAY-koh dee bee-AHN-koh)   **DOC**   Bianco is a small town on the coast just about under the "big toe" of Calabria Region, about 25 kms from the inland town of Gerace. Much of the wine made here in the past has been known as Greco Di Gerace. It is an excellent dessert wine made from the Greco grape, *passito*, up to 19% alcohol, very smooth and delicate — about *abboccato* or *amabile* on the scale when young, but turns more amber and gets drier with age. Very small production.

GRECO DI GERACE

(GRAY-koh dee jair-AH-chay)   See above.

GRECO DI TODI

(GRAY-koh dee TOH-dee)   The Greco grape is used to make this wine in Todi, a small town on the Tiber River in Umbria Region; the wine is semi-dry and apt to be quite strong; drink it young. A very good rosé made here as well as an excellent Vin Santo.

GRECO DI TUFO

(GRAY-koh dee TOO-foh)   **DOC**   A fine white wine made from 80-100% Greco grapes or with a maximum of 20% Coda Di Volpe; Tufo is a small town near Avellino E of Naples in Campania Region; the wine is straw-colored, dry, soft, well-rounded, much better with a little age but drink it before three; it is better chilled; there is also a good *spumante* made here.

GRIGNOLINO

(GREE-no-LEE-noh)   Superior red wine grape and the wine made from it in Piedmont Region; over seven million liters made annually; ruby-red, dry, light- to medium-bodied, not made for aging; some very fine rosé is made from this grape, but it should be drunk before its first birthday.

GRIGNOLINO D'ASTI

(GREE-no-LEE-no DAHS-tee)   **DOC**   This grape makes a distinctive wine at Asti in Piedmont Region — with 10% Freisa grapes allowed; deep-red, dry, good flavor, medium-bodied. Serve with good red meat before it turns five years of age.

GRIGNOLINO DEL MONFERRATO CASALESE

(GREE-no-LEE-no del mohn-fair-RAH-toh kah-sah-LAY-sa) **DOC**
Excellent red wine from this grape with 10% Freisa allowed, made close to the
Asti area in Piedmont Region; ruby-red with orange tint developing as it ages,
dry, full-bodied, best at three years of age; serve with red meat.

GRILLO

(GREEL-loh)   White wine grape grown in Sicily Region and one of the basic
grapes in Marsala (see).

GROPELLO

(groh-PEL-loh)   (1)   Red wine grape grown in the Lake Garda area of
Lombardy Region and used in many rosé wines; DOC has been applied for,
for a zone to be Gropello della Valtenesi.   (2)   A good but light-bodied red
wine is made from this grape in the Trentino-Alto Adige Region.

GROSSONERO
(GROH-soh-NAY-roh)   Red wine grape grown in Sicily Region and used in Cerasuolo Di Vittoria (see).

GROTTAROSSSA
(GROHT-tah-ROHS-sa)   Good red, white and rosé wines made at Caltanisetta in Sicily Region; the red is from Nerello and Calabrese grapes; the white from Trebbiano plus others.

GRUMELLO
(groo-MEL-loh)   A town in the Valtellina Superiore (see) area of Lombardy Region, and the name of an excellent red wine made there from the Nebbiolo grape.

GUARNACCIA
(gwar—NAHCH-cha)   Good red wine grape grown in the Campania Region and used in Ischia and Capri wines.

GULLO
(JOOL-loh)   White wine grape grown in Sicily Region.

GUNCINA
(joon-CHEE-nah)   Good red wine made from the Schiava grape in the Isarco River valley in the Trentino-Alto Adige Region; the wine is deep-red, dry, soft, medium-bodied.

GUTTURNIO DEI COLLI PIACENTINI
(joot-TOOR-nee-oh day KOHL-lee pee-ah-chen-TEE-nee)   **DOC**   Very good red wine made from 60% Barbera and 40% Bonarda grapes in the Piacenza hills S of that city in the NW part of Emilia-Romagna Region; very dark red in color, made *secco*, *abboccato* and *amabile*, the first two need a little age (they peak at five) but drink the *amabile* young. A good *spumante* is also allowed. There are many good wines from Trebbiano, Bonarda and Barbera grapes made here that are not DOC. See Ziano.

92

H

Hardly used in the Italian alphabet.

HECTARE — ETTARO in Italian
(AYT-tahr-roh) A metric land measurement of 10,000 square meters — used somewhat as we use the term "acre"; the equivalent is 2.471 acres U.S.

HECTOLITRE — ETTOLITRO
(ayt-TOH-lee-troh) A metric term for 100 liters; the U.S. equivalent is 26.42 gallons.

HELLENICA
(AYL-lay-nee-ka) also "Hellicon." A grape known in ancient Greece and believed to be the ancestor of today's Aglianico.

HERCULANEUM
(air-kwa-LAH-nee-um) Ancient Roman city destroyed with Pompeii by an eruption of Mt. Vesuvius in 79 AD.

HIRPINIA
See Irpinia.

HORACE
(65-8 BC) Roman poet who wrote much about wines. Caecuban, Falernian, Sabinum, Calenium, Formian, Albanum, Massicum and Surrentum are some of those mentioned in his writings.

I

I. N. E. INSTITUTO NAZIONALE ESPORTAZIONE
(een-stee-TOO-toh nah-tzee-oh-NAHL-ah ays-por-TAH-tzee-OH-na) An organization formed years ago to set high standards of quality and purity for all wines exported to the U.S.. Wines so approved used a red seal on a neck label immediately below the lip of the bottle with the letters INE printed thereon. It is known loosely as the "Marchio Nazionale."

IESI
(ee-AY-see) We spell it "Jesi," but the letter "J" is almost obsolete in the Italian alphabet. Iesi is a small town in the Marche Region, near Ancona, where the famous wine — Verdicchio dei Castelli di Jesi is made. Most labels for export carry the letter "J" as a concession.

IMBOTTIGLIATO
(eem-boht-tee-lee-YAH-toh) Bottled, placed in the bottle. *Imbottigliato all'origine* — bottled at the origin; *imbottigliato nella zona di produzione* — bottled in the zone of production; *imbottigliato al castello* or *alla fattoria* — bottled at the castle or at the estate.

INFERNO
(een-FAIR-noh) One of the best of the red wines made from the Nebbiolo grape in the Valtellina Superiore (see) area of Lombardy Region; also "Hell" or hot.

INZOLIA
(enn-TZOH-lee-ya) White wine grape grown in Sicily Region; used in Corvo, Marsala and other wines.

IRNO
(EER-noh) Ordinary wines, red and white, dry and sweet, made near Salerno in the Irno valley, Campania Region; they can be quite strong and should be drunk young.

IRPINIA
(eer-PEEN-ya) An area E of Naples, Campania Region, close to Avellino, where wines have been made since the Roman era; sound, inexpensive, carafe wines that are constantly being improved.

BIANCO

(bee-AHN-ko)   is made from Code Di Volpe/Trebbiano/Greco grapes; dry, medium-bodied, best served cold, with fish, and drunk young.

ROSATO

(roh-SAH-toh)   is from 50% Sanginoso, 50% Aglianico/Piedirosso and other grapes, for a good dry rosé, to be drunk young; see Lacrimarosa.

ROSSO

(ROHS-soh)   is made from 50% Sanginoso, 50% Anglianico/Piedirosso/ Sangiovese/Barbera grapes; ruby-red, dry, medium- to full-bodied; peaks at about five years.

ISARCO

(ee-SAHR-koh)   River in the NE section of the Trentino-Alto Adige Region, draining much of that area, joining the Adige River close to Bolzano. The name is EISAK in German; see Valle Isarco for wines.

ISCHIA

(EES-kee-ah)   **DOC**   Wines made on this small island in the Bay of Naples, Campania Region, for hundreds of years.

BIANCO

(bee-AHN-koh)   is straw-colored, dry, pleasant carafe wine made from 65% Forastera, 20% Biancolella and others; drink it young.

BIANCO SUPERIORE

(bee-AHN-ko soo-pay-ree-OHR-ay)   is similar to the above but uses only 50% Forastera/40% Biancolella and 10% San Lunardo grapes, for a richer, rounder, better wine; drink before its second birthday.

ROSSO

(ROHS-soh)   This red wine is made from 50% Guarnaccia, 40% Piedirosso and 10% Barbera grapes, ruby-red, dry and light-bodied; drink before its third birthday.

ISERA

(ee-SAY-rah)   A small town in the Trentino-Alto Adige Region and a very good rosé made there from the Marzemino grape.

ISOLA

(ee-soh-lah)   Island.

ISONZO

(ee-SOHN-zoh)   **DOC**   The Isonzo is a river rising in the Alps and flowing mostly S, past the city of Gorizia and emptying into the Gulf of Trieste east of Aquileia. The Region is Friuli-Venezia Giulia; the wines were consumed locally for many years until recent expansion now allows for exports. They are all excellent-to-superior; the varieties are shown on the labels and each wine must be 90% of that variety.

CABERNET

(kah-bear-NAY)   A typical wine from this grape, but a little lighter, needs age; medium to full-bodied, ruby-red and dry; best age is from 5 to 8 years.

MALVASIA ISTRIANA

(mal-vah-SEE-as ees-tree-AH-na) The Istrian peninsula juts into the Adriatic Sea and is the source of this name — Istriana; the wine is a typical, straw-colored, light-bodied wine from the Malvasia grape, with a hint of spiciness.

MERLOT

(mair-LOW) From the Merlot grape, a ruby-red, dry, soft, medium-bodied wine, a little lighter here, at its best at two years of age and to be drunk before it is five.

PINOT BIANCO

(PEE-noh bee-AHN-koh) An excellent wine from the Pinot Bianco grape, straw-colored, light-to medium-bodied, dry; try it as an aperitif but drink it young.

PINOT GRIGIO

(PEE-noh GREE-jee-oh) An excellent white wine, not as dry as the Pinot Bianco, good body; again, a good aperitif to be drunk young.

RIESLING RENANO

(REES-ling ray-NAHN-oh) From the White Riesling grape, straw-colored with a greenish tint, dry, medium-bodied, good flavor.

SAUVIGNON

(soh-veen-YONH) is from the Sauvignon grape, deeper straw-colored, dry, flowery bouquet, medium-bodied, best in its first year.

TOCAI

(toh-KIE) This grape does so well in this Region — a dry, smooth wine with good body, sometimes with a slight almond flavor, best in its first year.

TRAMINER AROMATICO

(trah-MEE-nair ahr-oh-MAH-tee-koh) Straw-color, aromatic, medium-dry, slightly bitter; drink young.

VERDUZZO

(vair-DOOTZ-tzoh) Golden-yellow, fruity, dry and slightly sweet versions made; also a Ramandolo — a dessert wine.

ISSOGNE

(Fr: ee-SOHN) See Vin d'Issogne.

ISTRIA

(EES-tree-ah) Large mountainous peninsula extending into the Adriatic Sea at its N end; it was part of the Austro-Hungarian Empire until the end of WWI, and after WWII, the scene of many bloody clashes with the Yugoslavs; Trieste, a very busy port was awarded to Italy with the bulk of the territory going to Yugoslavia.

ITALIA

(see-TAHL-ya) Italy, as they spell it!

J

JERZU or YERZU
(YAIR-tzoo) Brand name for excellent wines made in the small town of Jerzu in the north end of Sardinia Region; the grape is the Cannonau and the red wine is dry, full-bodied, strong (15%), a very good example of the wines this grape will produce; there is also a good *rosato* produced here.

JESI
(YAY-see) See Iesi.

K

KALTERN, KALTERER, KALTERERSEE, KALTERERSEEWEIN
Under the Austrians (prior to WWI) the town of Caldaro was Kaltern, the wine from it was Kalterer; Lago di Caldaro (Lake Caldaro) was Kalterersee, and the wine from the lake area Kaltererseewein. The Region is Trentino-Alto Adige. See Caldaro. The area is bi-lingual and both languages are often seen on the label.

L

L'AQUILA

(la-KWEE-lah)   City of 30,000 people, Capitol of the Abruzzo Region.

LA   CHIESA

(lah-kee-AY-sa)   is translated "the church"; this is a good wine made from 70% Pinot Bianco, 20% Nebbiolo and 10% Riesling grapes, in the Sondrio area — the Valtellina — in the N part of Lombardy Region.

LACRIMA   CHRISTI

(lah-KREE-ma KREE-stee)   also spelled "Lacryma." These two words are a fantasy name translated "tears of Christ" and, as such, on a wine label, can mean anything — or nothing, whether the wine comes from Mt. Vesuvius, Calabria or any other Region. Here are two stories about the area of Mt. Vesuvius: when Lucifer was thrown from Heaven, he grabbed a piece as he fell, and it became Naples; when the Lord discovered it, He wept and His tears landed on Mt. Vesuvius, creating vines where they fell! A second involved the return of Jesus to Earth and when He visited Naples, He was so shocked at their sinful way of living, He wept and vines sprouted from where His tears fell on Mt. Vesuvius. (Take your pick!)

LACRIMA CHRISTI DEL VESUVIO
(lah-KREE-mah KREE-stee del vay-SOO-vee-ch)   Various sources have reported that this DOC went into effect in 1979 but the list dated July 1, 1981, from the DOC Committee in Rome did not include this wine. It is understood (by the author) that the DOC zone will be named Vesuvio with a sub title of the above name. There is a *bianco*, a *rosato* and a *rosso* made. See Vesuvio for more detail.

LACRIMA DI CASTROVILLARI
(lah-KREEM-ah dee kah-stro-veel-LAHR-ee)   A dry red wine made and consumed in this town in Calabria Region.

LACRIMAROSA D'IRPINIA
(lah-KREEM-ah-ROH-sa deer-PEEN-ya)   Excellent rosé made from the Aglianico grape in the Irpinia (see) area; good rosé color, dry and medium-bodied. Candidate for DOC.

LAGO DI CALDARO
(LAH-go dee kahl-DAHR-oh)   KALTERERSEE.   A beautiful small lake on the outskirts of Bolzano, in the Trentino-Alto Adige Region. See Caldaro for wines.

LAGO DI COMO
(LAH-go dee KOH-moh)   Lake Como — to us; a very famous resort area around this spectacularly beautiful lake in the NW part of Lombardy Region; it is about 30 miles long and very deep, as are most lakes in the craters of extinct volcanos.

LAGO DI CORBERA
(LAH-go dee kor-BEAR-ah)   A small lake between Todi and Orvieto in Umbria Region; many good wines mostly from Trebbiano and Sangiovese grapes are made in the area.

LAGO DI GARDA

(LAH-goh di GAHR-da)   This lake is on the E side of Lombardy Region, with its head in Trentino-Alto Adige Region; it also forms part of the boundary of Veneto Region and Lombardy Region and is Italy's largest — some 40 miles long, and very deep. The area has always been famous for the fine rosé wines made here for centuries.

LAGO MAGGIORE

(LAH-go mahj-JOHR-ay)   Another large lake, also in Lombardy Region, with its head in Switzerland; also part of the boundary with Piedmont Region. The Swiss Alps rise majestically to the N and the plains of Lombardy stretch from the S end of the lake to the Po River.

LAGO TRASIMENO

(LAH-go trah-see-MAY-noh)   is about five miles W of Perugia; some very good red and white wines are made in the area including Colli del Trasimeno (see). The Region is Umbria.

LAGREIN

(lah-GRAIN)   Good red wine grape grown in the Trentino-Alto Adige Region; see Trentino and Alto Adige for wines.

LAGREIN SCURO

See Alto Adige.

LAMBRUSCO

(lahm-BROOS-koh)   Red wine grape, of which several varieties exist, grown mostly in the Emilia-Romagna Region; some plantings exist in Trentino-Alto Adige Region and there is a good Lambrusco made near Mantua in the Lombardy Region. It is certainly one of Italy's best-known wines, if not one of the best, and has been made since the Roman days. In the opinion of the author, Riunite Lambrusco (a brand name) has done for Italian wines (and wines in general) what the Gallo brothers have done for California wines (and wines in general)!! An interesting note is that even though the wine has been castigated by wine-lovers (?), the medical profession says that this wine has a

greater anti-cholesterol effect than any other red wine. So, if you like fatty foods...! Modena is at the center of this trade. All of these wines, including the many, many brand names, are substantially the same − a common ruby-red to purple in color, semi-dry, fruity, *frizzante*, and should be drunk young and fresh; a great amount of rosé is made. The DOC zones are named with no attempt to show percentages of grapes:

LAMBRUSCO DI PARMA
See Colli Di Parma.

LAMBRUSCO DI SORBARA
(lahm-BROOS-koh dee sohr-BEAR-ah) **DOC** Sorbara is a small town N of Modena; this supposedly is the best of the Lambruscos made; there is often a bouquet of violets.

LAMBRUSCO GRASPAROSSA DI CASTELVETRO
(lahm-BROOS-koh grahs-pahr OHS-sa dee KAHS-tell-VAY-tro) **DOC** What a long name to hang on the neck of a simple wine! *Grasparossa* are the red grape stalks and Castelvetro the town; this one (and others) made both dry and sweet.

LAMBRUSCO REGGIANO
(lahm-BROOS-koh rayj-jee-AH-noh) **DOC** This is a small town N of Modena and the wine is often almost pink in color and generally has more bubbles.

LAMBRUSCO SALAMINO DI SANTA CROCE
(lahm-BROOS-koh sahl-ah-MEEN-oh dee SAHN-ta KRO-shay) **DOC** Still another type of grape − *Salamino* refers to the slight salami-shape of the grape; Santa Croce is a small village.

LAMEZIA
(lah-MAY-tzee-ya) **DOC** Lamezia is a small town S of the Savuto River in Calabria Region; the wine is made from 30-50% Nerello, 25-35% Gaglioppo, 25-35% Red Grecco and other grapes.

LANCELLATTA
(lahn-chayl-LAHT-tah) Common red wine grape grown heavily in the Emilia-Romagna Region and used in many Lambruscos; also a red wine by that name.

LANGHE HILLS
(LAHN-gay) A range of hills SE of Turin in Piedmont Region, home of many fine red wines.

LANUVIA HILLS
(lahn-NOO-vee-ya) Hills near Lake Albano in the area S of Rome, Lazio Region, known as the Castelli Romani (see).

103

LATISANA

(lah-tee-SAH-nah) **DOC** Latisana is a town on the Tagliamento River, SW of Udine, in the Friuli-Venezia Giulia Region where wines have been made since the Roman Era; mostly consumed locally with little left for export; fortunately for us, this picture is beginning to change. They are all from very good to excellent, are labeled varietally, and must be 90% of the variety.

CABERNET

(kah-bear-NAY) Either of the two Cabernet grapes may be used in this zone producing a typical wine of its type — ruby-red, dry, a little softer than some, full-bodied, excellent. Peaks at five to eight years.

MERLOT

(mair-LOW) As in the other zones, there is a tremendous acreage in Merlot grapes here, producing a fine, soft, dry, ruby-red wine that peaks at four years.

PINOT BIANCO

(PEE-noh bee-AHN-koh) Excellent, full-bodied, dry, smooth, drink it young.

PINOT GRIGIO

(PEE-noh GREE-jee-oh) More golden in color than the Pinot Bianco, but a very good, dry, smooth, soft wine.

REFOSCO

(ray-FOHS-koh) Ruby-red with a purple edge, tannic, dry, needs three years of age, slightly bitter after-taste.

TOCAI FRIULANO

(toh-KIE free-oo-LAHN-oh)) A light yellow, dry, light-bodied wine with a slightly bitter after-taste; excellent for "quaffing."

VERDUZZO

(vair-DOOTZ-tzoh) is golden-yellow, dry, fruity and full-flavored.

LATIUM

Another name for Lazio.

LAZIO

(LAH-tzee-oh) Large Region of 6634 square miles of central Italy, bounded on the N by Tuscany and Umbria Regions, on the E by Abruzzo Region, on the SE and S by Molise and Campania Regions, and on the W by the Tyrrhenian Sea. It is probably more famous as the location of Rome, the Capitol of the Region as well as Italy; about five million population, quite mountainous and many small lakes; the Tiber River flows through Umbria before entering Lazio Region on its way through Rome and to the sea; the famous Pontine Marshes were drained in the 1930s and now, under the Aprilia name, are producing superior red wines; the Alban Hills have furnished the everyday wine to the citizens of Rome for 2000 years; home of many DOC wines (see Appendix) and others for a healthy annual production of 500 million liters.

LAZIO REGION

LESSONA

(lays-SOH-na)   **DOC**   Fine red wine named for a small town in the Novara Hills area of Piedmont Region; made from the Nebbiolo grape with 25% Bonarda added; red to garnet, full-bodied, smooth and dry; two years is the minimum age and it is often good for twenty more!

LEVERANO

(lay-vair-AH-noh)   **DOC**   A small town about one mile E of Copertino in the Salento peninsula, Puglia Region.

BIANCO

(bee-AHN-koh)   is from 65% Malvasia, maximum of 35% Bombino/Trebbiano, straw-colored, semi-dry.

ROSATO

(ros-SAH-toh)   is from 65% Negroamaro, 35% Malvasia/Sangiovese/ Montepulciano and others; typical rosé color, dry.

ROSSO

(ROHS-soh)   65% Negroamaro, 35% Malvasia/Sangiovese/Montepulciano and others, ruby-red, dry, full-bodied, slightly bitter after-taste, a *riserva* is available.

LIGURIA

(lee-GOO-ree-yuh)   One of the smallest, and certainly one of the most beautiful Regions of Italy, 2089 square miles in area, two million people, the Capitol is the famous city of Genoa. Named for the ancient peoples — the Ligurii, it was part of Cesalpine Gaul in Caesar's time. After the Fall of Rome, and many invasions, the struggle for control was mostly between the City-State of Genoa and the feudal lords, with Genoa winning in the 15th Century and retaining control until is was annexed to the Kingdom of Sardinia (Savoy — Piedmont) in 1815. This area, the Italian Riviera, is so beautiful from its beaches to the Alps rising so majestically in the background, and has found the tourist business so rewarding, that the wine production has fallen slowly over the years to about 40 million liters annually. The best-known wines are Cinqueterre and Dolceacqua, both DOC; see also Barbarossa, Coronata, Lumassina and Pigato.

GENOA

SAN REMO

LA SPEZIA

LIGURIA REGION

LIMBADI

(leem-BAH-dee)   Small village on the W coast of Calabria Region producing an ordinary red wine of this name, harsh, strong, made both dry and sweet.

LIPARI ISLANDS

(LEE-pahr-ee)   Seven small volcanic islands off the NE tip of Sicily, also known as the Aeolian Islands — in Greek mythology, the home of Aeolus, god of winds, and Vulcan, god of fire. Stromboli has an active, constantly erupting volcano some 3000 feet high.

LIQUOROSO

(lee-kwoh-ROH-soh)   A very sweet dessert wine, usually made from a *passito* wine and fortified with brandy.

LISON

(lee-SOHN)   A small town in Veneto Region noted for a very good table wine — Tocai di Lison (see). Continue reading:

LISON — PRAMAGGIORE

(lee-SOHN-prah-mahj-JOHR-ay)   is the name of a new proposed DOC zone centered around Portogruaro, between the Livenza and Tagliamento Rivers, N and E of Venice. It will contain the existing DOC wines of Cabernet Di Pramaggiore, Merlot Di Pramaggiore and Tocai Di Lison. Others to be included are a Malvasia, a Pinot Bianco, a Pinot Grigio, a Raboso, a Refosco, Riesling Italico and Riesling Ranano, a Sauvignon, and a Verduzzo. This may be approved in 1981.

LITRI

(LEE-tree)   A liter; the closest U.S. equivalent is 33.875 ounces; there are 3.787 liters in one U.S. gallon.

LOCOROTONDO

(loh-koh-roh-TOHN-doh)   **DOC**   A small town between Bari and Brindisi, Puglia Region; the wine is made from 50-65% Verdeca, 35-50% Bianco D'Alessano and other grapes for a straw-colored, dry, good carafe wine similar to the Martinafranca; much good *spumante* is made here; drink the table wine before it is three years old.

LOMBARDIA

(LOHM-bar-dee-yuh) Or Lombardy as we spell it. A large land-locked Region of 9189 square miles, 8½ million people, Capitol city is Milan; bordered on the N by Switzerland, on the E by Trentino-Alto Adige and Veneto Regions, on the S by Emilia-Romagna Region and on the W by Piedmont Region. The area was a battlefield for centuries, named for the Lombards and the center of their kingdom after the Fall of Rome and highly prized by all of the invaders. Milan and Venice fought for control for many years; later the Spanish and Austria ruled the area until it was liberated at the beginning of the Risorgimento. It is a beautiful mountainous area, with glaciers in the Alps, small yet spectacular lakes, much Medieval architecture in its cities. The inhabitants have always been industrious, hard-working people. The average annual wine production is about 225 million liters and the best-known wine areas are the Valtellina, Oltrepò Pavese and Lake Garda.

LUCANIA

(loo-KAHN-ya) Ancient Greek name for the area known today as the Basilicata Region; the name came from the ancient inhabitants — the Lucanii.

LUCCA

(LOOK-kah) City of 45,000 people, N and E of Pisa in the Tuscany Region; after Rome fell, it was part of a Lombardian Duchy, later a Free City and still later part of the Duchy of Parma. There is much fine Medieval architecture standing.

LUGANA

(loo-GAH-nah) **DOC** A small town near Lake Garda, Lombardy Region, and the home of a delightful white wine made from 90% Trebbiano grapes; straw-colored to gold, fresh, soft, medium-bodied, will hold its age for two or three years; an excellent wine with fish.

LUMASSINA

(loo-mahs-SEE-na) An interesting white wine made from the Lumassina grape in Liguria Region; straw-colored with a greenish tint, made *secco*, *amabile* with a slightly bitter after-taste, and a very good *spumante*. Drink the still wine young!

LUSARDO or LUXARDO

A brand of fruit wines (and spirits) made in the Veneto Region and packaged in many different designs of small decanters holding to about six ounces.

108

LOMBARDY REGION

Lambrusco
DI MODENA
rosa

VINO FRIZZANTE ROSATO

imbottigliato all'origine da: Unione Cantine Sociali S.C. a R.L.
Cittanova (Modena) ITALIA – 712/MO

72 cl   alcool effettivo 10% vol. – totale 10,50% vol.   **FL**

M

MAESTRI
(my-ESS-tree)   Good red wine grape grown in Emilia-Romagna Region and used in some Lambrusco wines.

MAGLIOCCO
(mah-lee-OHK-koh)   Another name for the Gaglioppo grape grown in Calabria and Sicily Regions; also a wine by this name in Calabria Region.

MAGNA GRAECIA
(mahn-ya GRAY-sha)   The Greek name for their colonies in Italy, founded between 800 and 1000 BC; they covered approximately the southern half of the Peninsula; their decline coincided with the rise of the Roman Empire about the 5th Century BC.

MAGO
(MAH-go)   A gentleman-farmer of Carthage, author of a treatise on agriculture, translated into Greek and Latin, used extensively by Italians in the 2nd and 3rd Centuries BC, as farming became "big business." One' writer has referred to him as "The Father of ALL Agriculture."

MALBEC also **MALBECK** and **MALBEK**
The superior red wine grape probably transported to Italy from the Bordeaux area of France sometime early in the 19th Century; it has not been widely planted but it is found occasionally mixed with the Cabernet grapes.

MALVASIA
(mal-vah-SEE-ah)   White wine grape famous since the dawn of history; probably brought by the Greek colonists to Italy c. 1000 BC. It is of the Muscat family and grows from the Aosta Valley all the way through to Sicily, and is generally made as a sweet table wine or dessert wine, vinified dry in a few instances, also a *spumante* and a *liquoroso*; a red variety exists but is not widely grown.

MALVASIA DE NUS
See Malvoisie de Nus.

111

MALVASIA DELLE LIPARI
(mal-vah-SEE-ah del-la LEE-par-ee) **DOC** Lipari is one of the islands in that group off the NE tip of Sicily Region; it produces, according to many experts, the best of the dessert wines from this grape (here, a slightly different variety); it is golden, rich, sweet, but a very small production. The *passito* must be 18% and a *liquoroso* is made at 20% alcohol.

MALVASIA DI BOSA
(mal-vah-SEE-ah dee BOH-sa) **DOC** From the town of Bosa near Nuoro in Sardinia Region comes this rich, golden, full-bodied, strong (15%), dessert wine from the Malvasia grape; there is a *secco* and a *dolce naturale*; two fortified versions are made: *liquoroso secco* and *liquoroso dolce naturale* which are at least 17½% alcohol. The best comes from the Planargia Mountains but there is very little made.

MALVASIA DI CAGLIARI
(mal-vah-SEE-ah dee KAHL-yar-ee) **DOC** There is a slight almond taste to this group of four wines made near Cagliari in Sardinia Region; two are made with 15% alcohol, generally *secco*, but also a *dolce naturale*; two are made fortified: *liquoroso secco* and *liquoroso dolce naturale*, 17½%, which may carry *riserva* if aged for two years after fortification.

MALVASIA DI CASORZO D'ASTI
(mal-vah-SEE-ah dee kah-SOHR-tzoh DAH-stee) **DOC** These two towns, Casorzo and Asti, are in the S part of Piedmont Region; the wines are different in that they are *rosato* and *rosso* from 90% Malvasia and 10% Freisa/Grignolino/Barbera; the color can vary but both wines are aromatic, sweet and *frizzante*; a *spumante* is allowed.

MALVASIA DI CASTELNUOVO DON BOSCO
(mal-vah-SEE-ah dee kah-stel-noo-OH-voh dohn BOHS-koh) **DOC** Another red Malvasia which allows 15% Freisa to be added to the Malvasia; the color is cherry-red, typical aroma and sweet taste; both *frizzante* and *spumante* made; Castelnuovo is a town in the Piedmont Region.

MALVASIA DI GROTTAFERRATA
(mal-vah-SEE-ah dee GROHT-tah-fayr-RAH-tah) A good amber, rich, sweet dessert wine made from the Malvasia grape near the town of Grottaferrata SE of Rome, Lazio Region.

MALVOISIE DE NUS
(Fr: MAL-vwah-zee dee NOOS) A sweet, strong (17-18%), dessert wine from the Malvasia grape, made in the town of Nus by the local priest who is also a winemaker — high in the Aosta Valley (Region). Candidate for DOC.

MAMERTINE — MAMERTINO
(mah-mair-TEE-no) Ancient wine made in Sicily and described by Plato as a great favorite in Rome about 150 BC; still made today around Mt. Etna from Catarratto/Grillo/Inzolia grapes; white, dry, better with a little age; there is an *amabile* made — both versions are strong.

MAMMOLO

(MAHM-moh-loh)　Red wine grape grown in Tuscany Region.

MANDROLISAI

(mahn-droh-lee-SIE)　**DOC**　From the central part of Sardinia Region, near Nuoro, and made from 50% Bovale, 25% each of Cannonau and Monica grapes, this wine is made in *rosato* and *rosso*; the *rosato* is an excellent rosé, dry, with a slightly bitter after-taste; the *rosso* is a clear ruby-red, also dry, same after-taste, better with a little age, a *superiore* is available.

MANTONICO

(mahn-TOH-nee-koh)　White wine grape grown in the Calabrian Region and the wine made from it; quite strong (16%), sweet when young but turns dry with several years in wood. Also grown in Sicily Region and used in some of their wines.

MARANI

(mah-RAH-nee)　Common red wine grape grown in Emilia-Romagna Region and used in some Lambrusco wines.

MARCHE

(mahr-KAY)　Region of 3740 square miles in area, 1½ million people, Capitol city of Ancona, on the Adriatic side of the Peninsula, bordered on the N by Emilia-Romagna Region, on the E by the Adriatic, on the S by Abruzzo and on the W by Umbria − the central part of Italy. The ancient name was Picenum; settled by the Greeks and considered their "back door" by the Romans; the name comes from the German word "mark" and was a part of the Empire of Charlemagne who gave it to the Church; part of the Papal States (see) prior to the Risorgimento. Always a very poor region in its economy, it is beginning to "come to life." Verdicchio dei Castelli di Jesi is its most famous wine in a total annual production of about 230 million liters.

MARCHE REGION

114

MARCHIO NAZIONALE See I.N.E.

MAREMMA

(mah-RAYM-ma)   The large coastal plain on the W side of Tuscany Region from Pisa in the N to Grosseto in the S; much very good white wine is made here and has been for many centuries. See Ardenghesca.

MARINO

(mah-REE-noh)   Town S of Rome, Lazio Region, near Lake Albano, producing red, white and rosé wines for 2000 or more years; they are made all ways — dry, semi-dry and sweet, still and sparkling. See next entry and Castelli Romani.

MARINO BIANCO

(mah-REE-nah bee-AHN-koh)   **DOC**   From 25-55% Trebbiano, to 75% various Malvasias, to 10% Bonvino/Cacchione grapes, fruity and soft; made *secco*, *amabile* with a *superiore* available and also a *spumante*, quite sweet. These wines have been improved tremendously in the last 20 years. See above.

MARSALA

(mahr-SAHL-ah)   **DOC**   Named for a seaport of 85,000 people on the westernmost point of Sicily Region, this wine is another of the fine wines produced in Italy. The Arabs, who conquered Sicily in the 9th Century, named this fine harbor "Marsa Allah" or "harbor of God." The wine is known throughout the world and was first made in the 1700s by English producers as an alternate to Oporto wines (Port) from Portugal; the grapes are 85% Catarratto and Grillo with 15% Inzolia allowed; it is then fortified and made in four basic styles:

1) Marsala *fine*, also labeled IP for Italy Particular, is at least 17% and ranges from dry to sweet — shown on the label — probably the least expensive.

2) Marsala *superiore*, minimum 18%, aged two years before release (and good until it is ten), ranging from dry to sweet as indicated on the label. This is the kind generally shipped to the U.S. It may also be labeled LP for London Particular, SOM for Superior Old Marsala and GD for Garibaldi Dolce (supposedly the favorite of the hero of the Risorgimento).

3) Marsala *vergine* is 18%, dry and must be aged for five years; it is seldom seen in this country.

4) Marsala *speciale* is a *superiore* with various flavors such as egg particles (*all'uovo*), almonds, etc. There were several highly flavored Marsalas in this country in the 1950s and 1960s but they have, like many innovations, almost disappeared. Bananas, coffee, oranges and strawberries have no place in Marsala — in the opinion of this author!

While the production and consumption of this wine declined in the 1930s and 1940s, it is again on the increase with almost 38 million liters made annually. Don't overlook its use in your kitchen — a bottle should be handy to the stove! Some evening try it with a bit of soft Gorgonzola — it is superb!

MARTINA or MARTINAFRANCA

(mar-TEEN-ah-FRAHN-kah)   **DOC**   A small town in Puglia Region gives its name to this wine from 50-65% Verdeca, 35-50% Bianco D'Alessano and 5% others, the same grape percentages as in Locorotondo — and very similar in taste; it has a greenish cast, pleasant, dry, light-to-medium body, drink it before it is three; a *spumante* is also allowed.

MARZEMINO

(mahr-tzay-MEEN-oh)   (1)   Excellent red wine grape grown in Trentino-Alto Adige and Tuscany Regions;   (2)   also a good dry, full-bodied red wine, and a good rosé made in the Alto Adige area.

MASSARDA

(mahs-SAHR-da)   A good white wine made W of San Remo in the Liguria Region; drink it young, before its first year.

MATINO

(mah-TEE-noh)   **DOC**   Named for a small town in the Salento Peninsula, Puglia Region, near Gallipoli on the Ionian coast, this wine is one of the "comers" of southern Italy; the DOC does not permit a *bianco*; both the *rosato* and *rosso* are from 70% Negroamaro and a maximum of 30% Sangiovese/Malvasia; the color varies, naturally, but both wines are dry, light to medium-bodied and well-balanced.

MELISSA

(may-LEES-sah)   **DOC**   This wine is named for this town near Ciro in the central part of Calabria Region; there are two wines:

BIANCO

(bee-AHN-koh)   is made from 80-90% Greco, 5-20% Trebbiano/Malvasia grapes; straw-colored, delicate and dry.

ROSSO

(ROHS-soh)   The grapes are 75-95% Gaglioppo, 25-5% Greco/Trebbiano and others; the color varies from rosé to a ruby-red, dry, and full-bodied; a *superiore* is available.

MELLOW

Not a DOC-defined term; used on some labels shipped to this country at the whim of the shipper or importer; it generally indicates a semi-sweet wine — about *amabile* on the scale.

MERANESE DI COLLINA

(mair-ah-NAY-sa dee kohl-LEE-na)   MERANER HUGEL or MERANER **DOC**   This ruby-red wine comes from the Merano hills in the N part of the Adige River valley in the Trentino-Alto Adige Region; it is made entirely from the Schiava grape, very good, dry, light- to medium-bodied, softens with age. Burgravio may appear on the label if from that zone.

MERANO

(mair-AH-noh)   Small town in the upper part of the Adige River Valley about ten miles from the Austrian border.

MERLOT

(mair-LOW) Famous red wine grape probably transplanted from Bordeaux in the early 1800s; excellent to superior wines are being made from this grape in Italy, particularly in the Trentino-Alto Adige, Veneto and Friuli-Venezia Giulia Regions; it is probably about one-half the total planted in the Friuli; the wine it makes is soft, easy to drink, soon ready; softer than the wines from the Cabernet grapes and often mixed with them for that reason; it also grows well on flat lands and is producing excellent wine in Aprilia.

MERLOT DI APRILIA

(mair-LOW dee ah-PREE-lee-ya) **DOC** A superior red wine made 100% from the Merlot grape in the Aprilia area S of Rome in Lazio Region; dry, soft, fruity, well-balanced, excellent with red meats.

MERLOT DI PIAVE

See Vini Del Piave.

MERLOT DI PRAMAGGIORE

(mair-LOW dee prah-mahj-JOHR-ray) **DOC** A superior red wine made from 90% Merlot and 10% of either of the Cabernet grapes, in the area around this town N of Venice in the Veneto Region; it is dry, soft, very well-balanced; a *riserva* is available. As with most Merlots, drink it before it is five with red meats. There is a new DOC zone proposed for this area to be called Lison-Pramaggiore (see).

MERLOT TRENTINO

See Trentino.

MESSINA

(mays-SEE-na) (1) narrow strait of water separating Sicily from the mainland of the Peninsula; (2) the 3rd largest city in Sicily, a seaport of 250,000 people that was 90% destroyed in the 1908 earthquake; (3) the source of the ancient wine — Messinan — a favorite of Rome.

METAURO

(may-TOHR-oh) Small river rising in the Apennines and flowing E, entering the Adriatic Sea about ten miles S of Pesaro, the Marche Region. See Bianchello del Metauro.

METODO CHAMPENOIS

(may-toh-doh shahm-payn-WAH) Italian for the process of making Champagne in France — fermented in the bottle — the classic method.

MILANO

(mee-LAHN-oh) Or Milan as we call it — Capitol of the Lombardy Region, 2 million people, the richest industrial city in Italy. In history, capitol of the Duchy of Milan; many examples of Medieval architecture remain including the famous Cathedral started in the 14th Century, also the home of the prestigious La Scala Opera.

MILO

(MEE-loh) Small town in Sicily Region important to the Mt. Etna wine trade.

MISSANTO

(mee-SAHN-toh) White wine made in Liguria Region; straw color, very dry, a good "quaffing" wine; also made *amabile*; best in its first year.

MODENA

(MOH-day-na) A very old city in Emilia-Romagna Region; seat of the Duchy of Modena from the 13th Century until the Risorgimento; today an important center of the Lambrusco trade.

MOLINARA

(moh-lee-NAH-rah) Excellent red wine grape grown in Veneto Region and used in Bardolino and Valpolicella wines.

MOLISE

(moh-LEE-sa)   One of the smaller of the twenty administrative Regions into which Italy is divided; 1715 square miles in area, 300,000 population, Capitol city is Campobasso in the south central part; bounded on the N by Abruzzo Region, on the E by the Adriatic Sea, on the S by Puglia and Campania Regions and on the W by Campania and Lazio Regions; part of the Papal States (see) immediately prior to the Risorgimento. Quite mountainous and little-traveled, it is one of the "coming" areas, albeit slowly; few wines are bottled and labeled, let alone exported — one such is San Barbato (see); several producers are working on their wines for DOC recognition. Montepulciano and Sangiovese are the grapes used for most of the red wines with Trebbiano and others for the white wines.

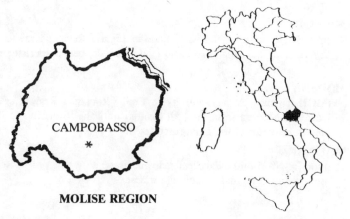

CAMPOBASSO
*

MOLISE REGION

MONDRAGONE

(mohn-dra-GOH-nay)   Small town near Caserta in Campania Region where good Falerno and Falernum wines (see) are produced.

MONFERRATO

(mohn-fair-RAH-toh)   A hilly area covered with vineyards around the town of Asti, E and SE of Turin, Piedmont Region; source of some of Italy's finest red wines.

MONICA

(MOH-nee-ka)   Red wine grape grown in Sicily and Sardinia Regions and used in their wines.

MONICA DI CAGLIARI

(MOH-nee-ka dee KAHL-yar-ee)   **DOC**   A rich, smooth, red dessert wine made near the city of Cagliari, Sardinia Region, from 100% Monica grapes; a *passito* wine, some say it reminds them of Malaga, strong (15%), made both *secco* and *dolce naturale*; there are also two fortified wines made with 17½% alcohol — *liquoroso secco* and *liquoroso dolce naturale*; the two *liquoroso* types are available in a *riserva* with an additional two years of age.

MONICA DI SARDEGNA

(MOH-nee-kah dee sar-DAYN-ya)   **DOC**   This red wine differs from the above Monica Di Cagliari in that 15% other grapes are allowed; it is dry, made all over Sardinia Region, full-bodied, and a *superiore* is available. Peaks at about seven or eight years.

MONTAGANA

(MOHN-tah-GAH-nah)   Small village in the central part of Molise Region making a good red wine of this name from the Montepulciano grape.

MONTAGNA

(mohn-TAHN-ya)   Good red wine made in the Valtellina area of the Lombardy Region.

MONTALBANO

(mohn-tahl-BAHN-oh)   One of the seven areas where Chianti is made; this one ages well and often has an aroma of violets (see Chianti).

MONTALCINO

(mohn-tahl-CHEE-noh)   (1)   Small town in the Siena Hills of Tuscany Region, home of the famous Brunello Di Montalcino wine (see).   (2)   A vineyard area near Lake Trasimeno in Umbria Region producing good *rosato* and *rosso* wines from the Sangiovese grape; also a good wine from the Moscato grape; all three are candidates for DOC.

MONTE ANTICO

(MOHN-tay ahn-TEE-koh)   Excellent red wine made in the Maremma area, Tuscany Region, from 80% Sangiovese, 20% Canaiolo/Ciliegiolo/Trebbiano grapes; ruby-red, getting a little lighter with age, slightly tannic, smooth and velvety; at its peak at four to five years.

MONTE CONERO

See Rosso Conero.

MONTE DONATO

(MOHN-tay doh-NAH-toh)   A red wine made in the Emilia-Romagna Region.

MONTE GIOVE
(MOHN-tay JOH-vay) Brand name for a red Orvieto wine (yes!) made in Umbria Region; included here for that reason.

MONTE SAN PIETRO
(MOHN-tay SAHN pee-AY-troh) See Colli Bolognesi.

MONTECARLO BIANCO
(mohn-tee-KAHR-loh bee-AHN-koh) **DOC** Small town E of Lucca in Tuscany Region producing this wine from 60-70% Trebbiano, 30-40% Semillon/Pinot Grigio/Pinot Bianco/Vermentino/Sauvignon/Rousanne! A straw-yellow, dry, smooth, very good wine in its first year. There is a *rosso* made here from Chianti grapes but not DOC.

MONTECOMPATRI — COLONNA or
MONTECOMPATRI or COLONNA
(mohn-tay-kohm-PAH-tree — koh-LOH-na) **DOC** All names allowed. These two towns about 15 miles SE of Rome, Lazio Region, produce a white wine from a maximum of 70% Malvasia and 30% Trebbiano, with an allowable 10% of Bellone/Bombino grapes; straw-colored, good carafe wine, made both *secco* and *amabile*; a *riserva* is available.

MONTEFALCO
(mohn-tay-FAHL-koh) **DOC** This town is S of Assisi in Umbria Region. There is no *bianco*.

ROSSO
(ROHS-soh) Excellent red wine from 65-75% Sangiovese, 15-20% Trebbiano, 5-10% Sagrantino, etc; ruby-red, dry, full-bodied, smooth with a little age to dispel the tannin, best age is about three years.

SAGRANTINO
(sah-grahn-TEEN-oh) has been made here for hundreds of years from this grape, now a 5% maximum of Trebbiano is allowed; the wine is ruby to garnet and has a flavor of blackberries; rich and smooth, sometimes *frizzante*; a *passito* at 14% is allowed and is even sweeter. The production is very small but the wine is well worth looking for.

MONTEFIASCONE
See Est! Est!! Est!!!

MONTEGABBIONE
(mohn-tay-gahb-bee-OH-nay)   A small town near Orvieto in Umbria Region producing an excellent dry rosé from the Sangiovese grape, best in its first year.

MONTELLO E COLLI ASOLANI
(mohn-TAY-loh ay KOHL-lee ah-soh-LAHN-ee)   **DOC**   This zone is in the hills of Asolo and Montello just S of the Piave River near the town of Monte-belluna in Veneto Region. Note the difference in naming the wines:

CABERNET
(kah-bear-NAY)   is an excellent red wine from this grape, dry, full-bodied, smooth and velvety; a *superiore* is available.

MERLOT
(mair-LOW)   is made from all Merlot grapes, ruby-red, dry, smooth, full-bodied, ready to drink, a *superiore* is made.

PROSECCO
(proh-SEK-koh)   is a still wine made from the Prosecco grape, straw-colored, dry, fruity, slightly bitter after-taste; of the tremendous amount of this wine made, most of it is as a *spumante*, a superior sparkling wine — made in three degrees of sweetness — *brut*, *abboccato* and *dolce*; best in the *abboccato* style.

NOTE: There is an excellent white wine made from the Pinot Grigio grape, but not yet DOC. See also Venegazzu.

MONTEPULCIANO
(mohn-tay-pool-CHAH—noh)   (1)   A good red wine grape grown heavily in Abruzzo, Molise, Puglia and other Regions with many local wines made from it; generally needs a little age;   (2)   a small town in Tuscany Region producing one of Italy's best red wines — Vino Nobile Di Montepulciano — but not made from Montepulciano grapes!

MONTEPULCIANO D'ABRUZZO

(mohn-tay-pool-CHAH-noh dah-BROOTZ-tzoh) **DOC** Excellent red wine made near Pescara in the Abruzzo Region, from 85% Montepulciano grapes with 15% Sangiovese allowed; deep red when made, with an orange tint as it ages; a *vecchio* with two years, better with four or five; it has been much improved in the last twenty years but still will vary among wineries; about 20 million liters made annually.

MONTEPULCIANO DEL MOLISE

(mohn-tay-pool-CHAH-noh del moh-LEE-sah) Good red wine from this grape made all over the Molise Region; ruby-red tending to purple with age, dry, full-bodied, robust, needs to breathe for several hours; a *rosato* is also made — dry and fresh. Candidates for DOC.

MONTERICO

(mohn-TAY-ree-koh) Common red wine grape grown in Emilia-Romagna Region.

MONTEROSSO VAL D'ARDA

(mohn-tay-ROHS-so val DAHR-da) **DOC** The Arda Valley is S of Piacenza in Emilia-Romagna Region and produces this white wine from 30-50% Malvasia, 10-30% Moscato Bianco, 20-35% Trebbiano with an allowable 20% Bervedino/Sauvignon; straw-colored, Muscat bouquet, it will vary in taste; made *secco*, *amabile*, *frizzante* and all best drunk young; excellent with pork meats; a fine, dry, light *spumante* with a wonderful fresh taste is also made.

MONTESANTO

(mohn-tay-SAHN-toh) Ordinary red wine made from Montepulciano and Sangiovese grapes, in the Marche Region; ruby-red and slightly sweet.

MONTESCUDAIO

(mohn-tay-skoo-DAH-yo) **DOC** From Livorno, or Leghorn as we call it (why?), a fine port in the N part of Tuscany Region on the Tyrrhenian Sea, come three wines:

BIANCO

(bee-AHN-koh) is from 75-80% Trebbiano, 15-30% Malvasia/Vermentino, 10% other grapes; straw-colored and dry — a good carafe wine.

ROSSO

(ROHS-soh) is from 65-85% Sangiovese, 15-25% Trebbiano/Malvasia plus 10% other grapes; deep ruby-red, dry, soft and fruity; needs a little age for smoothness.

VIN SANTO

(veen SAHN-toh) is made from Trebbiano/Malvasia grapes, smooth, strong (14% +), aged for three years and has a slightly bitter after-taste.

MONTUNI DEL RENO

(mohn-TOO-nee del RAY-noh) Excellent white wine made near Parma in Emilia-Romagna Region; from Montuni grapes, straw-colored, pleasantly fresh, in several styles: *secco*, *abboccato* and *amabile*, both still and *spumante*; best served cool, young, and with lighter meats. Candidate for DOC.

MORASCA

(mohr-AH-ska) This wine comes from near Savona in Liguria Region; gold-to-amber in color, dry, made from 80% Bianchetta grapes with some Vermentino and Trebbiano; drink it before its first birthday.

MORELLINO DI SCANSANO

(mohr-el-LEE-noh dee skahn-SAHN-oh) **DOC** From the town of Scansano in the SW corner of Tuscany Region; this red wine is made from 85-100% Sangiovese grapes, ruby-red, quite dry, needs age to dissipate the tannin; a *riserva* is available.

MORI VECIO

(MOHR-ee-VAY-cho) Brand name for an excellent red wine made from 50% Cabernet Sauvignon and 50% Merlot grapes in the Trentino-Alto Adige Region; dry, robust, needs three years of age; peaks about ten depending somewhat on the vintage; excellent with hearty red meats.

MOSCATO — MOSCATO BIANCO

(moh-SKAH-toh bee-AHN-koh) Italian for Muscat; a Moscato Bianco is any white Muscat wine. This grape is planted all over Italy and has many sub-varieties; one finds it from the Aosta Valley through Sicily, made from *amabile* to *dolce*, still and *spumante*; most of them have a similar Muscat aroma and taste. One might well be advised that wherever one goes in Italy, THAT place is the ONLY place that makes a true Moscato — all the rest are poor imitations!

MOSCATO D'ASTI or MOSCATO D'ASTI SPUMANTE
MOSCATO NATURALE D'ASTI
ASTI SPUMANTE or ASTI
SPUMANTE BRUT — not a DOC zone as the others are.

Since there seems to be confusion in the minds of many, these four titles are combined at this point to clarify the differences among them without the technicalities in the *disciplinari* — the legal description as approved by the DOC Committee:

MOSCATO NATURALE D'ASTI

(moh-SKAH-to nah-toor-AHL-uh DAHS-tee) **DOC** is a white, STILL table wine, slightly sweet, made from Moscato Bianco grapes, generally the Moscato Di Canelli, in a delimited area near the towns of Asti and Alessandria in the Piedmont Region.

MOSCATO D'ASTI or MOSCATO D'ASTI SPUMANTE
(moh-SKAH-toh DAHS-tee / spoo-MAHN-tee) **DOC**
ASTI SPUMANTE or ASTI
(AHS-tee spoo-MAHN-tee) **DOC** These two DOC wines are SPARK-LING wines made from the STILL wine — Moscato Naturale D'Asti. The Charmat (bulk) process is used; both are *dolce* on the scale and the Moscato D'Asti Spumante is generally sweeter than the Asti Spumante. All of these wines range in color from white to straw to gold; all have the typical Muscat bouquet and taste, and should always be served cold.

SPUMANTE BRUT
(spoo-MAHN-tee BROOT) is "a horse of a different color"!! It is an entire-ly different wine — made from the Pinot family of grapes, by the classical method of fermentation in the bottle; it is dry, fruity and clean, sometimes with a slight bitterness; generally aged for three years or more and the vintage must be shown on the label. It is always a wine of very high quality. The terms "nature" and "brut" are used as they seem to possess close to the same meaning in all the languages of wine.

MOSCATO D'ELBA

(moh-SKAH-toh DELL-bah) From the island of Elba off the Tuscan coast (Tuscany Region) comes a fine dessert wine — the volcanic soil giving a different taste to the Moscato grape — the wine is sweet and strong (15%).

MOSCATO DELL'OLTREPÒ PAVESE

See Oltrepò Pavese.

MOSCATO DI CAGLIARI

(moh-SKAH-toh dee KAHL-yar-ee)   **DOC**   A smooth, sweet dessert wine from the Moscatello, the local name for the Moscato Bianco grape or a very close cousin, around Cagliari in the Sardinia Region; almost gold in color, strong (15%), typical Muscat bouquet and taste, and called *dolce naturale*; a fortified type — *liquoroso dolce naturale* — is made at 17½% alcohol with a *riserva* available.

MOSCATO DI CANELLI

(moh-SKAH-toh dee kah-NAYL-lee)   The Moscato Bianco grape (or a close cousin) as grown around the town of Canelli and highly desirable for Asti Spumante (see).

MOSCATO DI COSENZA

(moh-SKAH-toh dee koh-SEN-tzah)   White Muscat wine made around the town of Cosenza in the central part of Calabria Region; typical Muscat aroma and taste, sweet, strong (17%), dessert wine.

MOSCATO DI NOTO

(moh-SKAH-toh dee NOH-toh)   **DOC**   The small town of Noto in Sicily Region produces this very good, sweet dessert wine from the Moscato grape, gold to amber in color; there are three types: a still table wine, a *spumante* quite sweet, and a fortified *liquoroso* with a minimum of 22% alcohol. The annual production is very small.

MOSCATO DI PANTELLERIA NATURALE or
MOSCATO DI PANTELLERIA
(moh-SKAH-toh dee pahn-tel-LAY-ree-ah) **DOC** Pantelleria is a small volcanic island between Sicily and the coast of Africa, part of the Sicily Region; the grape is the Zibibbo or Moscatellone, a variety of the Muscat grape; the wine is gold to amber, typically Muscat, strong (17%), a *vino naturalemente dolce*; there is a *spumante* and a *liquoroso*. See also Moscato Passito Di Pantelleria.

MOSCATO DI SALENTO
(moh-SKAH-toh dee sah-LEN-toh) is a dessert wine made on the Salento Peninsula, Puglia Region, from the Moscato grape; typical bouquet and taste, gold in color, sweet and strong (17%).

MOSCATO DI SARDEGNA
(moh-SKAH-toh dee sahr-DAYN-ya) **DOC** A *spumante* from the Moscato Bianco grape, almost gold in color, about *amabile* on the scale, made almost all over the island and Region of Sardinia.

MOSCATO DI SIRICUSA
(Moh-SKAH-toh dee seer-ee-KOO-sah) **DOC** Another dessert wine from the Moscato Bianco grape made near Syracuse in Sicily Region; dark gold, typically Muscat, at least 16½% alcohol, quite sweet. Legend says it was made by King Pollius in the 7th Century BC, who came from Greece. The annual production is very small.

MOSCATO DI SORSO-SENNORI or
MOSCATO DI SORSO or **MOSCATO DI SENNORI**
(moh-SKAH-toh dee SOHR-so sayn-NOR-ee) **DOC** All names are allowed. Sorso and Sennori are two small towns in the N part of Sardinia Region; the wine is typically Muscat, golden yellow, rich, sweet, 15% alcohol; a fortified style — *liquoroso dolce* is also made.

MOSCATO DI TRANI
(moh-SKAH-toh dee TRAH-nee) **DOC** From the town of Trani, NW of Bari in Puglia Region, comes this sweet, smooth, golden wine from the Moscato Bianco grape; here the grapes are slightly dried; there are two kinds produced: *dolce naturale* with 15% alcohol and a fortified *liquoroso* with at least 18% alcohol.

MOSCATO DI ZUCCO
(moh-SKAH-toh dee TZOOK-koh) is a sweet, strong, golden dessert wine from the Moscato Bianco grape made near the town of Zucco in Sicily Region.

MOSCATO GIALLO
(moh-SKAH-toh JAHL-loh) A yellow Muscat grape grown in many places all over Italy.

MOSCATO NATURALE D'ASTI
(moh-SKAH-toh nah-too-RAL-ay DAHS-tee) **DOC** This is a STILL
white wine from the Moscato Bianco grape made in the Piedmont Region,
from which Asti Spumante is made. See Moscati D'Asti for fuller explanation
and clarification.

MOSCATO PASSITO DI PANTELLERIA or
PASSITO DI PANTELLERIA
(moh-SKAH-toh pahs-SEE-toh dee pahn-tel LAY-ree-ah) **DOC** A *passito*
wine from the Zibibbo, a variety of the Moscato family of grapes, made on
the island of Pantelleria off the coast of Sicily — and part of that Region; it
has the typical Muscat bouquet and taste, is a minimum of 14% alcohol and
very sweet. A fortified *liquoroso* of at least 21½% is made; if it reaches 24%,
has been aged for an additional year and is bottled and sold on that island, the
term *extra* may be shown on the label.

MOSCATO TRENTINO
See Trentino.

MOTTALCIATA
(MOHT-tahl-chee-AH-ta) A very fine dry red wine, full-bodied, made from
the Nebbiolo grape in Piedmont Region.

MT. ETNA
See Etna for wines.

MT. VESUVIUS
The Italians call it *Vesuvio* (see).

MT. VULTURE
An extinct volcano in Basilcata Region; see Aglianico del Vulture.

MULLER — THURGAU
Well-known white wine grape from Germany — now thought to be a cross
between two Riesling grapes — for many years thought to be a cross of
Riesling and Sylvaner; grown to a limited extent in N Italy; see Alto Adige
and Valle Isarco.

NAPOLI

(NAH-poh-lee)   We call it Naples: the Capitol of the Region of Campania, population of 1½ million, important port and tourist center — the city closest to Capri, Mt. Vesuvius and Pompeii. Years ago it was the third largest city in Europe after London and Paris; its decline started after the Risorgimento; seat of the Kingdom of Naples and the Kingdom of The Two Sicilies. Garibaldi and King Victor Emmanuel II met outside the city in 1861, completing the Unification of Italy except for the seizure of Rome in 1870. The area was settled by Greek colonists and has been producing wines ever since.

NASCO

(NAHS-koh)   White wine grape grown in Sardinia Region; believed to have been brought there by the Spaniards.

NASCO DI CAGLIARI

(NAHS-koh dee KAHL-yar-ee)   **DOC**   Four wines are made from the Nasco grape around the city of Cagliari in Sardinia Region; starting with the grapes slightly raisined, they are a *secco* and a *dolce naturale*, both about 15% alcohol, two fortified types both over 17½% alcohol, called *liquoroso secco* and *liquoroso dolce* and may be labeled *riserva* with two more years in wood; straw-colored, slightly bitter after-taste, peaks about five or six years of age; annual production less than 25,000 liters.

NEBBIOLO

(nayb-bee-OH-lo)   Superior red wine grape known to have been growing in 1300 in northern Italy — the Piedmont Region — where it does so well producing so many of Italy's finest reds; Barolo, Barberesco, Carema, Gattinara, Ghemme and also called the Spanna there; known as the Picoutener in the Valle D'Aosta and as the Chiavennasca in Lombardy Region. More DOC wines are produced from this one grape than any other. There is also a great amount of wine labeled simply "Nebbiolo" — excellent wines requiring only three to five years of age, dry, full-bodied, and also made *amabile*, *spumante*, *rosato*, and even some *bianco* (yes!). The average annual production is estimated at 17 million liters.

NEBBIOLO D'ALBA

(nayb-bee-OH-lo DAHL-bah)   **DOC** Excellent red wine from the Nebbiolo grape near the town of Alba in Piedmont Region; ruby-red, full-bodied, slightly tannic; there is a *secco*, an *amabile* and a *spumante*; the *secco* must have one year of age before release; drink it before its fifth birthday although it may last longer.

NEBBIOLO DEI ROERI

(nayb-bee-OH-lo day ROAR-ee)   Excellent red wine made from the Nebbiolo grape in the Roeri Hills area of Piedmont Region. There is a Bianco Dei Roeri, a white wine from the Nebbiolo, made here also. Candidate for DOC.

NEBBIOLO DI RETORBIDO

(nayb-bee-OH-lo dee ray-tohr-BEE-doh)   This is a sweeter wine, about *amabile* on the scale, made from the Nebbiolo grape near the town of Retorbido in the Pavia area of Lombardy Region.

Granduca
Nebbiolo d'Alba
denominazione d'origine controllata

Imbottigliato nella zona di produzione da   Cantine Duca d'Asti Calamandrana (Italia)

Produce of Italy
Red table wine
Alc. by vol. 12%   Net cont.
750 ml./25.4 Fl. oz.

IMPORTED BY KOBRAND CORPORATION SOLE U.S. IMPORTERS N.Y. N.Y.

NEGROAMARO

(NAY-gro-ah-MAHR-oh)   Good red wine grape grown in Puglia Region and used in many wines.

NERELLO

(nay-REL-loh)   Good red wine grape grown in Sicily Region and the wine made there from it.

NERO

(NAY-roh)   Dark or black. The Pinot Nero grape is what we know as the Pinot Noir.

NERO D'AVOLA

(NAY-roh DAH-voh-lah)   Good red wine grape grown in Sicily Region and used in many wines made there.

NICASTRO

(nee-KAHS-troh)   Small village E of Catanzaro, Calabria Region, making ordinary red and white wines by this name.

NICE

(NEES)   City on the French Riviera, but included here as it was a part of Piedmont, or Savoy, for many years until 1860; also the birthplace of the patriot Garibaldi.

NELLA

(NAYL-la)   loosely — "at" or "in"; seen on the labels in locating the bottling of that wine.

NIGRARA

(nee-GRAHR-ah)   also spelled Negrara; excellent red wine grape grown in Veneto Region and used in Bardolino and Valpolicella wines (see both).

NOSIOLA

(noh-see-OH-la)   White wine grape grown in Trentino-Alto Adige Region and supposedly a native there, used in Sorni wines and also bottled under this name.

NOVARA and NOVARA HILLS

(noh-VAHR-ah)   Town and hills covered with vineyards furnishing some of Italy's best wines; about 55 air miles NE of Turin close to the Lombardy border.

NURAGUS

(noo-RAH-goos)   (1)   White wine grape grown for centuries in Sardinia Region; the wine from it is white, dry and strong;   (2)   the name is from the curious cone-shaped towers built of stone and several stories high, dating as far back as the 18th Century BC (yes!), remnants of an ancient civilization about which nothing is known.

NURAGUS DI CAGLIARI

(noo-RAH-goos dee KAHL-yar-ee)   **DOC**   This wine has been made for hundreds of years in this area — Cagliari is the city, Sardinia the Region, the grapes are 85-95% Nuragus, to 15% Trebbiano/Vermentino/Clairette/ Semidano; straw-colored, dry, strong (15%), mostly consumed locally; average annual production about 20 million liters.

NUS

(NOOS)   Small town six miles E of Aosta in the Valle D'Aosta Region. It is famous for a fine Malvasia dessert wine made by the local priest for many years. See Malvoisie de Nus and Vin de Nus.

134

O

OLIENA
(oh-lee-AY-na) One of the many wines from the Cannonau grape, this is from the hill town SE of Nuoro, Sardinia Region; deep, deep red, almost black, full-bodied, robust, strong (16%), tannic, needs several years of age.

OLTREPÒ PAVESE
(ohl-TRAY-po pah-VAY-sa) **DOC** Large, important, productive area, triangular in shape, S of the Po River, at one time part of the old Kingdom of Piedmont, now part of the Lombardy Region. Annual production exceeds 15 million liters. There are ten DOC wines:

BARBARCARLO
(BAR-ba-KAR-loh)   is an excellent red wine from Barbera/Croatina/Ughetta/Uva Rara grapes, dry, full-bodied; one year of wood aging is required; peaks about four or five; the name is translated "Charles' beard".

BARBERA
(bar-BEAR-ah) is often labeled Barbera Dell'Oltrepò Pavese; from 90-100% Barbera grapes with 10% Bonarda allowed; this wine is deep red, dry, needs age, usually peaks before the Piedmont Barberas, but good until it is five.

BONARDA

(boh-NAHR-da)   is a deep-red, full-bodied, dry, soft wine, with about 10% Barbera added to the Bonarda grapes.

BUTTAFUOCO

(boo-ta-foo-OH-ko)   is another long-time favorite in Milan; the name is translated "spitfire"; it is made from Barbera/Croatina/Ughetta/Uva Rara grapes, deep red, dry, full-bodied and peaks about four years or so.

CORTESE

(kor-TAY-sah)   is an excellent white wine made from all Cortese grapes, straw-colored, dry, fresh-tasting, but drink it young.

MOSCATO

(moh-SKAH-to)   is from the Moscato Bianco grape, with its typical bouquet and taste, sweet, aromatic, a *spumante* is also made here.

OLTREPÒ PAVESE

(ohl-TRAY-po pay-VAY-sa)   is really a *rosso*; made from a maximum of 65% Barbera, 25% Croatina plus other grapes, usually quite dry, full-bodied and needs a little age.

PINOT

(PEE-noh)   is a most unusual formula in that it may be either a Pinot Grigio or a Pinot Nero! This does not seem to be consistent with defining wines and grapes under DOC. If the Pinot Grigio is used, the color is a straw-yellow, dry, medium-bodied wine, with a *spumante* made from it also. If the Pinot Nero is used, the wine is more of a *rosato* (and is often so labeled), dry, fresh, excellent Pinot Noir flavor, but drink it under two years of age.

RIESLING

(REES-ling)   may be made from either the Riesling Italico or the Riesling Renano; both grapes produce a dry wine, straw-colored, to be drunk before it peaks at four; a *spumante* is also allowed in this type.

SANGUE DI GIUDIA

(SAHN-gay dee JOO-da)   is a good red wine made from Barbera/Croatina/Ughetta/Uva Rara grapes; is generally sweeter and most often slightly *frizzante*. The name is translated "Blood of Judas."

ORISTANO

(oh-ree-STAH-noh)   A small town on the Tirso River, a few miles from the Gulf of Oristano on the W side of Sardinia island (and Region) — famous for its wine — Vernaccia di Oristano (see).

ORMEASCO

(or-mee-AHS-koh)   White wine made from the Ormeasco and Dolcetto grapes in Liguria Region since 1300 AD; straw-colored, dry and pleasant before it reaches its first birthday.

ORTRUGO

(or-TROO-go)   Good white wine grape grown in the Emilia-Romagna Region.

ORVIETO

(or-vee-AY-toh)   **DOC**   Orvieto is a small city of 10,000 in Umbria Region, famous for a magnificent cathedral as well as this wine. Made from 50-65% Trebbiano, 15-25% Verdello, 20-30% Grechetto, and up to 20% Malvasia grapes; it is light, smooth, a wonderful fresh taste, both *secco* and *abboccato*; the quality will vary slighty, but an excellent wine for luncheons, chicken and fish. There are about eight million liters produced annually; drink it before its third year; there is a *classico* zone. Some red Orvieto is made from the Sangiovese grape but it is not DOC. A very small part of the DOC zone lies in Lazio Region.

OSTUNI

(oh-STOO-nee)   **DOC**   This is a small town N of Brindisi in the Puglia Region, making two wines with names other than the traditional *bianco* and *rosso*:

BIANCO DI OSTUNI

(bee-AHN-koh dee oh-STOO-nee)   A very good carafe wine made from 50-85% Impigno, 15-50% Francovilla with a maximum of 10% Alessano/-Verdeca grapes; straw-yellow, light, dry and fresh; drink it young.

OSTUNI   OTTAVIANELLO

(os-STOO-nee oht-tah-vee-ahn-NEL-lo)   is a good red wine made from 85% Ottvianello, 15% Negroamaro/Malvasia and other grapes; the color varies from cherry-red to a light ruby-red, dry, medium-bodied; delicious with roast lamb; peaks at four years.

SPARKLING WINE PRODUCED AND BOTTLED IN ITALY

NET CONTENTS 750 ML   ALCOHOL 11% BY VOLUME

Castel La Volta

Vino Bianco Spumante

S.p.A. CANTINE DEI MARCHESI DI BAROLO · BAROLO (PIEMONTE)

Exclusive U. S. Importer MUSA, Inc. BALTIMORE, Md.

P

PADOVA – PADUA – PADUA HILLS

We call the city Padua; Italian is Padova; the city is W of Venice, famous in history and for a university started there in 1222; wines have been made in the hills for 2000 or more years.

PAGADEBITI

(pah-gah-DAY-bee-tee) (1) Ordinary white wine grape grown in Puglia Region, producing a heavy, full-bodied wine used much in the making of Vermouth; it has an interesting translation "it pays your debts." (2) The grape is also grown in Emilia-Romagna and used in the wine "Pagadebit."

PALERMO

(pah-LAIR-mo) Seaport, the largest city (660,000) and Capitol of Sicily Region, located on the N coast of the island; founded by the Phoenicians c. 800 BC; much Medieval architecture remains, including a beautiful cathedral started in 1185.

PALUMBO

(pah-LOOM-boh) Ordinary white wine grape grown in Puglia Region, producing a strong, full-bodied wine used in making Vermouth, and as a blending wine.

PAMPANUTO

(pahm-pah-NOO-toh)   Ordinary white wine grape grown in Puglia Region, used in Vermouth.

PANNARANO

(pahn-na-RAH-noh)   A red wine from Aglianico and Sangiovese grapes made in the Campania Region; purple-red, dry, medium-bodied, tannic when young, needing two or three years of age to soften.

PANTELLERIA

(pahn-tayl-LAY-ree-ya)   Small volcanic island about 30 square miles in area, some 70 miles S of Sicily; source of some very fine dessert wines; see Moscato.

PAPAL STATES

Formerly an independent area under the rule of the Popes; it included the E part of Emilia-Romagna, most of Umbria, the Marche and Lazio Regions. The nucleus started with bequests of land to the Pope in the 4th Century continuing through the 12th Century, although Papal authority was not very secure for the next 200 years; even then it was, as with much of Italy "here today, gone tomorrow." After the Napoleonic Wars, the Congress of Vienna in 1815 restored the lands to the Vatican, but they were all "annexed" to the Kingdom of Sardinia or Italy, during the Risorgimento. King Victor Emmanuel II finally seized Rome in 1870 and declared it the Capitol of all Italy. Pope Pius IX and his successors considered themselves prisoners of the Vatican until the issues were resolved by the Lateran Treaty in 1929. The Vatican is now a sovereign state within the boundaries of the City of Rome.

PARADISO

(pair-ah-DEE-so)   Excellent red wine from the Nebbiolo grape made in the Valtellina area of Lombardy Region; named for the castle (now in ruins) built on the rock known in the area as *Il Paradiso*, NE of Sondrio; ruby-red, dry, full-bodied, generally aged three or four years before release. See also Valtellina Superiore.

PARMA

(PAHR-ma)   City of 75,000 in the NW part of Emilia-Romagna Region; seat of the former Duchy of Parma; center of the Parmesan cheese trade.

PARRINA

(pahr-REE-nah)   **DOC**   Two wines made near the Orbetello Peninsula in the SW corner of Tuscany Region, also labeled La Parrina:

BIANCO

(bee-AHN-koh)   is a good carafe wine made from 80% Trebbiano and 20% Ansonica/Malvasia Grapes; straw-colored, dry, with a slightly bitter after-taste.

ROSSO

(ROHS-soh)   is ruby-red, dry, big, smooth (with age) from 80% Sangiovese and to 20% Montepulciano/Canaiolo/Colorino grapes; aged one year before release and much better with three.

PARTINICO

(par-TEE-nee-ko)   Town near Palmero, Sicily Region, and the wines made there. The *bianco* is a big strong (16%), dry wine reputedly aged for 8 to 10 years! The *rosso* is also a big strong, dry red wine.

PASSITO

(pahs-SEE-toh)   A sweet wine made from partially dried or raisined grapes; sometimes the grapes are dried in the sun, more often in the attics of the houses, before pressing and fermenting. Years ago they were hung in the kitchens and the resulting wine had almost a smoky taste from the fire.

PASSITO DI CHAMBAVE

(pahs-SEE-to SHAHM-bahv) Chambave is a small town in the Aosta Valley (Region) producing an interesting, strong (15%), dessert wine from *passito* Moscato grapes; it turns dry after several years in the casks and is one of the very finest of dessert wines; candidate for DOC.

PAVIA

(pah-VEE-ah) City of 50,000 people, S of Milan, close to the junction of the Ticino and Po Rivers in Lombardy Region; a capitol of the old Lombardy Kingdom; famous since Medieval times as a center of learning — a law school and university were started in the 11th Century; also the center of the Oltrepò Pavese wine trade.

PELIGNA BIANCO

(pay-LEEN-ya bee-AHN-koh) Good white carafe wine made from various grapes in the town of this name, N of Sulmona on the Sagittario River in the Abruzzo Region.

PELLAGRELLI

(payl-lah-GREL-lee) Ordinary wines made near Caserta, Campania Region, *bianco*, *rosato*, *rosso* — all dry and medium-bodied.

PELLARO

(payl-LAHR-oh) Red wine made from the Nerello and Nocera grapes S of Reggio Calabria, in the tip of the Calabria Region; made both dry and sweet and needs age.

PER' 'E PALUMMO

(PAYR-ay pah-LOOM-mo) Good red wine grape, said to be the same as the Piedirosso, grown on the island of Procida, in the Bay of Naples, Campania Region; produces a good dry red wine best when very young.

PERDA RUBIA

(PAIR-da roo-BEE-ah) Brand name for an outstanding red wine made from the Cannonau grape near Nuoro in the Sardinia Region; deep red, rich, strong (17%), dry, full-bodied; a *rosato* is also made.

PERLA VILLA

(PAIR-la VEEL-la)   Brand name for an outstanding red wine from the Nebbiolo grape made in the Valtellina area of Lombardy Region.

PERPETUO

(pair-PAY-too-oh)   White wine made in Sicily Region.

PERRICONE

(payr-ree-KOHN-nay)   Red wine grape grown in Sicily Region and the wine made from it.

PERUGIA

(pay-ROO-jah)   City of 150,000 population, Capitol of and located in the N central part of Umbria Region; it contains a fine museum of Etruscana and an *enoteca* for Umbrian wines.

PESARO HILLS

(PAY-sahr-oh)   Small range of hills in the Marche Region; See Sangiovese Dei Colli Pesaresi.

PETIT ROUGE

(pay-TEE ROOZH)   Red wine grape grown in the Aosta Valley (Region) producing Enfer d'Arviers and other fine red wines with local names, including Torrette, Aymaville, Colline D'Aosta, St. Pierre, Sabla and others.

PETITE ARVINE

(pay-TEET ar-VEEN-ah)   Excellent red wine grape grown to a limited extent in the Valle D'Aosta Region.

PIACENZA HILLS

(pee-ah-CHEN-tzah)   Small wine area near the city of Piacenza in the W part of Emilia-Romagna Region. See Gutturnio Dei Colli Piacentini and Ziano.

PIAVE

(pee-AHV-ah)   (1)   A river rising in the Alps flowing mostly S through Veneto Region, some 140 miles long, emptying into the Adriatic E of Venice. (2)   A very important wine area E of Treviso; see Vini Del Piave for wines.

PICOLIT

(pee-koh-LEET)   A white wine grape grown in the Friuli-Venezia Giulia Region for over 1000 years; it produced a superb dessert wine treasured in the courts of Europe during much of the 19th Century. A disease decimated the vine and only in the last twenty years has the wine made a re-appearance — and that in extremely limited quantities as the yield is very low; probably less than 20 cases exported to this country annually. Most of that comes from Colli Orientali with some from Isonzo and a little from Emilia-Romagna. The wine is deep straw-yellow to amber, delicate bouquet, made from *passito* grapes.

PICOUTENER

(pee-KOO-ten-ay)   Local name in the French-speaking Valle D'Aosta for the Nebbiolo grape.

PIEDIROSSO

(pee-ay-dee-ROHS-so)   Red wine grape grown on Mt. Vesuvius and used in Lachrima Christi and Taurasi, Campania Region.

PIEMONTE

(pee-ay-MOHN-tay)   We call it Piedmont. A large, land-locked Region of 9817 square miles, 4½ million people, the NW corner of Italy, bounded on the N by Valle D'Aosta and Switzerland, on the E by Lombardy, on the S by Liguria and on the W by France and the Valle D'Aosta; the Capitol city is Turin. Part of the old Lombard Kingdom, it has been known as Savoy since the 11th Century. In 1720 the Duke of Savoy exchanged his claim to Sicily for Sardinia and took as his title — King of Sardinia. Much more territory was included — Nice, much of the French province of Savoie, the Aosta Valley and Liguria, but the present boundaries were finally established after World War II. King Victor Emmanuel II and his Prime Minister, Count Cavour, were certainly the nucleus of the Risorgimento as Garibaldi was the spark who set it afire! Today the Region is highly industrialized, and also the most important wine Region of Italy — producing the finest reds — Barolo, Barbaresco, Barbera, Grignolino, Freisa, and superior whites — Cortese, Asti Spumante, etc., for an average annual production of 450 million liters. There are many wine roads in the Region. Turin is the birthplace of bread sticks and Vermouth.

PIGATO

(pee-GAH-toh)   Good white wine from the Pigato grape made in Liguria Region for over 200 years; light gold, dry, fruity, slightly bitter after-taste; drink in its first year. Candidate for DOC.

PIGLIO

(PEE-lee-oh)   Small town SE of Rome, Lazio Region, and the good white wine made there for centuries; always known simply as Piglio, its name since DOC is Cesanese Del Piglio (see).

PIGNATELLO

(peen-ya-TEL-loh)   Good dry red wine made from the Pignatello grape in the W part of Sicily Region.

144

1 — L. Maggiore
2 — Ticino R.
3 — Gattinara
4 — Carema
5 — Novara
6 — Caluso
7 — Turin
8 — Po River
9 — Alessandria
10 — Asti
11 — Alba
12 — Tanaro R.
13 — Gavi

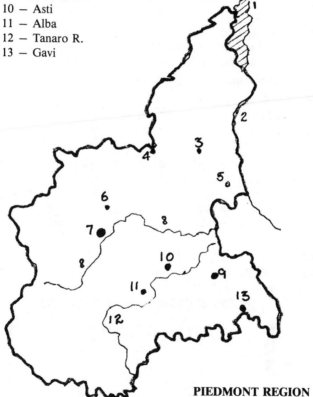

PIEDMONT REGION

PINOT BIANCO

(PEE-noh bee-AHN-ko)   The Pinot Blanc grape, as we know it, is grown mostly in northern Italy and produces fine wines, many of DOC status; it is mostly a dry, crisp wine excellent as an aperitif, with fowl and sea food. A large amount of *spumante* is also made from it.

PINOT CHARDONNAY

See Chardonnay.

PINOT GRIGIO

(PEE-noh GREE-jee-oh)   This is the Pinot Gris grape as we know it, grown mostly in NE Italy, producing fine wines, many of which are DOC, and much good *spumante*. The wine it produces is usually pale-yellow, light, dry and fruity but some make a wine with much more body and a deeper color; there is one version from Friuli — a copper color or *Ramato*.

PINOT NERO

(PEE-noh NAY-roh)   This is the Pinot Noir grape grown mostly in NE Italy and producing several excellent DOC wines; its German name in the Alto Adige area is Blauburgunder; much rosé is made from it.

PINOT TRENTINO

See Trentino.

PINOT DELL'OLTREPÒ PAVESE

See Oltrepò Pavese.

PISA

(PEE-sa)   City of 60,000 in NW Tuscany Region, formerly a port on the Tyrrhenian Sea but now separated by the delta of the Arno River; rich in history, one of the early Maritime Republics; defeated by Genoa in 1284 and by Florence in 1406; heavily bombed in WWII, but much Medieval architecture still stands, including a magnificent cathedral and the famous Leaning Tower of Pisa.

PITIGLIANO

(pee-tee-lee-YAH-no)   Small town in S part of Tuscany Region W of Lake Bolsena; see Bianco Di Pitigliano.

PLINY, THE ELDER

(23-79 AD)   Roman naturalist and writer who died while investigating the tremendous eruption of Mt. Vesuvius in 79 AD.

PO RIVER

(POH)   The longest river in Italy, rising in the W part of the Piedmont Region, flowing generally E to and through Lombardy, forming much of the boundary between Emilia-Romagna and its northern neighbors, emptying into the Adriatic Sea S of Venice, some 400 miles from its source.

POLCEVARA

(pol-chay-VAHR-ah)   Fine wines made for many years in Liguria Region, getting more scarce every year, or so it seems; the *bianco* is made mostly from the Vermentino grape, straw-colored, mellow, fresh-tasting, excellent when very young and served with fish; the *rosato* and *rosso* are made from Barbera and Sangiovese grapes.

147

POLLINO

(pohl-LEEN-oh) **DOC** Red wine named for the Pollino Mountains in the W central part of Calabria Region; from 60% Gaglioppo and at least 20% Greco/Malvasia with other grapes, it is ruby-red, dry, medium-bodied; there is a *superiore* available.

POMINO

(po-MEEN-oh) (1) Famous old name for a wine made in Tuscany Region long before Chianti was regulated. (2) Today a brand name owned by the Frescobaldi family who have been making two exceptional wines — a red using Cabernet Sauvignon with the Chianti grapes and a white from Pinot Bianco and Chardonnay. (3) A zone named Pomino is a candidate for DOC with three wines to be made: the red from 60-70% Sangiovese, 10-20% Cabernet Sauvignon/Franc, 5-10% Merlot, 5-10% Canaiolo plus other grapes; the white wine to be made from 60-80% Pinot Bianco/Chardonnay, 20-30% Trebbiano plus 10-15% other grapes; a Vin Santo is also included. Frescobaldi will renounce its exclusive right to Pomino when the DOC is approved.

PONTINE MARSHES

Hundreds of acres of once-swampy land S of Rome, Lazio Region, used as a buffer zone for centuries until drained in the 1930s; it is now producing some superior wines under the area name of Aprilia (see).

PORTOFINO

(pohr-toh-FEE-noh) White wine made from the Bosco and other grapes in the Liguria Region; straw-colored, dry, best in its first year, excellent when served cold with fish.

POTENZA

(poh-TEN-tzah) 25,000 people live in this Capitol city of the Basilicata Region; a serious earthquake created heavy damage in this area in November 1980.

PRAMAGGIORE

(prah-mahj-JOHR-ay) Town in Veneto Region, home of a large annual wine fair and two fine DOC wines made from the Cabernet and Merlot grapes. A new DOC zone has been proposed for this area to be called Lison-Pramaggiore (see).

PRIMITIVO

(pree-mee-TEE-voh) Red wine grape grown in Puglia Region; the name comes from "premature" since the grape matures in August, much earlier than most grapes; recent studies indicate it may be related to the Zinfandel of California.

PRIMITIVO DI GIOIA
(pree-mee-TEE-voh dee JOY-ya) Ordinary red wine from the Primitivo grape and the town of Gioia in Puglia Region; dark red, almost black, heavy, strong (18%), used for cutting and blending.

PRIMITIVO DI MANDURIA
(pree-mee-TEE-voh dee mahn-DOO-ree-yah) **DOC** A red table wine and three sweeter wines are made from the Primitivo grape in the town of Manduria in Puglia Region; red with orange tints as it ages, the *secco* is a full-bodied, strong (14%), well-balanced, smooth and velvety wine with proper age; the *amabile* is of course sweeter; the *dolce naturale* is 16% alcohol. There are two fortified *liquoroso* types made from the first above – a *liquoroso secco* with 18% or more alcohol and a *liquoroso dolce naturale* with at least 17½%; both must be aged for two more years; drink before they are six.

PROCANICO
(pro-KAH-nee-ko) Another name for the Trebbiano grape.

PROCIDA
(PROH-chee-da) One of the three islands (Capri and Ischia are the others) in the Bay of Naples, Campania Region; good red, white and rosé wines made and consumed locally.

PRODOTTO
(proh-DOHT-toh) Produced. PRODOTTORI Producer.

PROSECCO
(proh-sayk-koh) Excellent white wine grape grown in Veneto Region.

PROSECCO DI CONEGLIANO-VALDOBBIADENE or
PROSECCO DI CONEGLIANO or
PROSECCO DI VALDOBBIADENE
(pro-SAYK-koh dee koh-nel YAH-no / vahl-dohb-bee-AH-day-nah) **DOC** A very good white wine from these two towns in Veneto Region made with 90% Prosecco and 10% Verdiso grapes; almost white, light-bodied, dry, semi-dry, sweet, still, *frizzante* and *spumante*. Drink them young.
SUPERIORE DE CARTIZZE
(soo-pair-ee-OHR-uh dee kar-TEETZ-tza) contains an allowable 15% Pinot Bianco or Pinot Grigio; up to 25% of either of the two Pinot grapes is allowed in the *spumante* which is made both dry and semi-dry; annual production is between six and eight million liters.

PROVINCE – PROVINCIA
in Italian. The twenty Administrative Regions are divided into smaller areas called Provinces. Since many of these Provinces have the same name as the principal city within their boundaries, their names are eliminated from this volume to avoid confusion.

PUGLIA

(POOL-ya)   Also spelled Apulia. A Region of 7469 square miles in area — the "heel of the boot" and above; population about four million people, the Capitol is Bari; bounded on the N by Molise, on the E and S by the Adriatic Sea, and on the W by Basilicata and Lazio Regions; it has been called the "cellar of Italy." Settled by the Greeks, conquered by the Romans in the 4th Century BC, after the Fall of Rome by the Goths, Lombards, Byzantine Empire, Normans, Swabians, a Duchy under the Kingdom of Naples until the Risorgimento. Many fine ports including the Naval Base at Brindisi are on the Adriatic Coast; there is a fine cathedral in Foggia, and Bari is also noted as the resting place of the bones of Santa Claus. Puglians have always been considered beer drinkers, perhaps because their wines were such heavy blending wines and used in Vermouth and other wines. The table wine industry has developed tremendously in the last twenty years or since the inception of DOC. Look for continued improvements in the years to come. The average annual wine production is close to one billion liters. There are many DOC wines made here.

PUNT e MES

(POONT-ay-mess)   An aperitif with a wine base (similar to a Vermouth) and a rather bitter taste.

PUSTERLA

(poo-STAIR-lah)   Red, white and rosé wines made near the town of Lugana, Lake Garda area, Lombardy Region.

PUGLIA REGION

150

QUALITA
(kwal-EE-tah)   Quality.

QUANTITA
(kwan-TEE-tah)   Quantity.

QUATRO VICARIATI
(kwah-troh vee-KAR-ee-AH-tee)   A brand name for an excellent red wine — a blend of the two Cabernet grapes and 40% Merlot in normal years; made in the Trentino-Alto Adige Region; ruby-red, dry, medium-bodied, best drunk before its fifth birthday; it needs to breathe for an hour before serving with beef and other red meats. The label reads "4 Vicariati."

PRODUCT OF ITALY

VALDO®

NET
CONTENTS
750ML

PROSECCO
DI VALDOBBIADENE

ALCOHOL
11,5 %
BY VOL.

DENOMINAZIONE DI ORIGINE CONTROLLATA
V.S.Q.P.R.D.
SPARKLING WHITE WINE
BOTTLED BY VALDISO S.P.A. - VALDOBBIADENE - ITALIA
FOR VALDO S.P.A.
CERVIGNANO DEL FRIULI - ITALIA
IMPORTED BY P.L. IMPORTERS, INC., BROOKLYN, N.Y. 11205

R

RABOSO
(rah-BOH-soh)   Red wine grape grown in Veneto Region, and the wine made from it.

RABOSO DEL PIAVE
(rah-BOH-soh del pee-AH-va)   Red wine made from the Raboso grape in the Piave area of Veneto Region; strong, robust, dry, mouth-filling, needs three to five years of age to be its best.

RAMANDOLO
(rah-mahn-DOH-lo)   A sweet dessert wine made from the Verduzzo grape in Friuli-Venezia Giulia Region; see Colli Orientali del Friuli.

RAMITELLO
(rah-mee-TEL-loh)   A brand name for good wines made around Campomarino in the Molise Region:
BIANCO
(bee-AHN-koh)   is made from 85% Trebbiano and 15% Malvasia grapes; golden color, fruity but dry, serve cold and young.
ROSSO
(ROHS-soh)   is made from 70% Sangiovese and 30% Montepulciano grapes; ruby-red tending to purple with age, dry, smooth and velvety; needs to breathe for a few hours; has a slightly bitter after-taste; a *spumante* is also made.

RAPITALA

(rah-pee-TAHL-ah)   Rapitala is a small river in the W end of Sicily Region; this is a brand name from the Arabic meaning "Thanks be to God" (Allah); it is an Alcamo wine (see) fresh, dry and fruity, made from Catarratto and Trebbiano grapes.

RASPINOSO

(rah-spee-NOH-soh)   Red wine grape grown in the Tuscany Region.

RAVELLO

(rah-VAYL-loh)   Good wines made near Amalfi, S of Naples, Campania Region; the *bianco* is made from Greco/Ginestra/Fiano grapes; dry, medium-bodied; the *rosato* and *rosso* are made from Anglianico/Serpenteri/ Tintore and other grapes; medium-bodied, both dry and semi-dry.

RECIOTO

(ray-CHOH-toh)   A sweet dessert wine made from *passito* grapes of various kinds, all over Italy, and sometimes a *spumante*. Usually good for at least eight or ten years. Continue reading:

RECIOTO   DELLA   VALPOLICELLA

(ray-CHOH-toh del-la vahl-POL-ee-CHEL-la)   **DOC**   From Veneto Region, a deep red, heavy, sweet wine made from partially-raisined *superiore* grapes in the same formula as Valpolicella — 55-70% Corvina, 25-30% Rondinella, 5-15% Molinara and 10% others — full-bodied and smooth, made both dry and sweet; peaks about eight to ten years; the grapes may come from a *classico* zone in the Valpantena valley; a *liquoroso* and a *spumante* are also made.

AMARONE

(ah-mah-ROH-na)   is a dry version of this wine, similar to a light Porto although it has only 14% alcohol; it needs to breathe for about an hour.

RECIOTO   DI   GAMBELLARA

(ray-CHOH-toh dee gahm-bel-LAHR-ah)   **DOC**   White wine made from *passito* grapes of the Gambellara formula — 80-90% Garganega, to 20% Trebbiano, in the town of Gambellara near Verona in Veneto Region; gold in color, semi-sweet, a *spumante* is also made.

RECIOTO   DI   SOAVE

(ray-CHOH-toh dee SWAH-vay)   **DOC**   From the famous town of Soave, Veneto Region, and *superiore* quality of 70-90% Garganega, 10-30% Trebbiano grapes, *passito*, quite gold, semi-sweet and smooth; a *spumante* and a *liquoroso* are also made here.

REFOSCO

(ray-FOHS-koh)   Red wine grape grown in Friuli-Venezia Giulia Region, producing a ruby-red, dry, full-bodied wine that is rough when young but smooth when mature at eight to ten years depending on its vintage. It is reported that this vine is not affected by the phylloxera.

REGALEALI

(ray-gahl-ay-AHL-ee)   Excellent brand of wines made near Palermo, Sicily Region, extremely popular and very high quality; the *bianco* is made from Inzolia and Catarratto grapes, the *rosato* and *rosso* are made from Nero D'Avola/Nerello/Perricone grapes; both are dry and smooth, but the red is better with a little age.

REGGIO CALABRIA

(RAY-joh kahl-AH-bree-ah)   Port city of 70,000 people and Capitol of Calabria Region; located at the very "tip of the toe of the boot" on the Strait of Messina separating it from Sicily; it was almost destroyed by the 1908 earthquake.

REGIONE

(ray-jee-OH-nuh)   Region. There are twenty Administrative Regions in Italy, listed in the introduction and shown on the map on page 9.

RENANO

(ray-NAH-noh)   Italian for Rhine (river in Germany).

RIBOLLA

(ree-BOHL-la)   White wine grape whose origin is the Friuli-Venezia Giulia Region; used in Collio wines (see Colli Orientali) and occasionally mixed with Malvasia in that area.

RIESLING ITALICO – RIESLING RENANO

These two varieties of the famous White Riesling grape produce excellent-to-superior wines in northern Italy, perhaps better in Trentino-Alto Adige and Friuli-Venezia Giulia than elsewhere. They are seldom, if at all, made in the sweeter versions as in Germany; neither are they as classic as the Rheingau nor as flowery as the Moselle wines. One thing certainly in Italy's favor is that they do not permit the Sylvaner grape to be called a "Riesling," nor the Chauche Gris a "Grey Riesling," let alone the Missouri Riesling and others of like ilk – a practice deplored by the author.

RISERVA

Under DOC rules, a condition of age, different for different wines. On other than DOC wines it is a meaningless term and may be used to confuse the public.

RISERVA SPECIALE

(ree-SAIR-va spay-chee-AHL-ay) Under the DOC rules, a special period involving aging of a wine.

RISORGIMENTO

(ree-sor-jee-MEN-toh) The liberation of Italy from the domination of foreign powers during the period from 1859 to 1870 — also known as the unification of Italy.

RIUNITE

(ree-yoo-NEE-tee) Brand name for a Lambrusco sold more than any other in America. The sales have contributed tremendously in the orderly transition to drinking wine. See Lambrusco also.

RIVIERA — ITALIAN RIVIERA

The Region of Liguria — more particularly the seacoast; somewhat divided into the eastern and western sections with Genoa the central point.

RIVIERA DEL GARDA BRESCIANO

(ree-vee-AIR-ah del GAHR-da bray-SHAH-noh) **DOC** This zone has nothing to do with the Italian Riviera of Liguria Region; it is the zone name for the famous Lake Garda rosés and reds that so many visitors have enjoyed there for so many centuries. The Region is Lombardy; the grapes are 50-60% Gropello, 10-25% Sangiovese, 10-20% Barbera, 5-15% Marzemino; they vary slightly in taste but are delightful when fresh, cool and very young. Once experienced on a terrace overlooking the Lake, with a good luncheon, the taste will never be forgotten.

CHIARETTO

(key-ah-RET-toh) is a rosé, sometimes slightly sweet, sometimes a slight taste of almonds, drink it young and cool.

ROSSO

(ROHS-soh) is deeper in color than the rosé, dry, light to medium-bodied, better with a little age; a *superiore* is available.

RIVIERA *del* GARDA
BRESCIANO
DENOMINAZIONE D'ORIGINE CONTROLLATA

ROSSO
MAGUZZANO

IMBOTTIGLIATO NELLE CANTINE DI S. ZENO NAVIGLIO DA
PASINI ANDREA E FIGLI S.N.C.

0,75 litri   12 % vol

Soft, Semi-dry Red Wine

Riunite
LAMBRUSCO

CANTINE COOP. RIUNITE REGGIO EMILIA
Mellow Red Wine - Produce of Italy - Contents 1 Pt. 8 Fl. Oz. - Alc. 9% by vol

ROCCA DI PAPA

(ROHK-kah dee PAH-pah) A small town high on a hill in the Castelli Romani area outside of Rome, Lazio Region, with an excellent overall view of the City of Rome; the name is translated "rock of the Pope"; very good white wine made here, probably a mixture of Greco/Malvasia/Trebbiano grapes — a carafe wine.

ROMA

(ROH-ma) Or Rome as we know it — city of 2¾ million people; the Capitol of Italy and the Lazio Region, about 15 miles from the coast of the Tyrrhenian Sea. It is one of the richest cities in history and art, and one of the greatest cultural, religious and intellectual centers of the world. The Vatican City is a sovereign state within its borders. The tribes that inhabited its hills were subdued by the Etruscans about or before the 8th Century BC, who made a City-State there until overthrown by the Romans c. 500 BC in establishing the Roman Empire. After its disintegration, the area was overrun by countless aggressors until Papal authority became fairly constant in the 15th Century; even after that there were more invasions and often the Pope was on the short end. After the Napoleonic Wars, the Congress of Vienna restored the area to the Popes, who ruled until King Victor Emmanuel II and the new Italian Army seized the City in 1870 and declared it the Capitol of all Italy, thus ending the Risorgimento. Wines have been made in its environs for 2500 or more years.

RONDINELLO

(rohn-dee-NAYL-loh) Red wine grape of superior quality grown in the Veneto Region and used in Bardolino and Valpolicella wines.

ROSATO

(roh-SAH-toh) Rosé; any rosé wine; known also as Chiaretto (see) and Cerasuolo (see). There are many excellent ones (several DOCs) made all over Italy in the style of a fine light wine, rather than the rosé of transitional quality and type more familiar to Americans in the past two decades. See Bardolino, Castel Del Monte, Grignolino, Marzemino and Vin Ruspo.

ROSATO DEL SALENTO

(roh-SAH-toh del sah-LAYN-toh) A very good rosé, light and dry, made from Negroamaro/Malvasia/Ottavianello grapes in the Salento area of the Puglia Region.

ROSSANA

(rohs-SAH-nah) Another name for the Molinara grape grown in Veneto Region and used in Bardolino.

ROSSESE

(rohs-AY-sah) Excellent red wine grape grown in Liguria Region.

ROSSESE DI DOLCEACQUA

(rohs-SAY-sah dee dohl-chee-AH-kwa) **DOC** Superior red wine made from 95% Rossese around the town of Dolceacqua N of San Remo in Liguria Region; dry, medium-bodied, harsh when young, needs one or two years of age, peaks about four; a *superiore* is available.

ROSSIGNOLO

(rohs-see-YOH-loh)   Red wine grape grown in Sicily Region and the wine made from it.

ROSSO

(ROHS-soh)   Red — in Italian. *Vino Rosso* simply means any red wine.

ROSSO BARLETTA

(ROHS-soh bar-LAYT-ta)   **DOC**   Barletta is a port city on the Adriatic Coast of the Puglia Region; this wine is made from 70% Uva de Troia, 30% Montepulciano/Sangiovese/Malbec grapes, red, dry, needs age; an *invecchiato* with two years of age (one in wood) before release.

ROSSO CANOSA

(ROHS-soh kah-NO-sa)   **DOC**   This zone is near Bari in Puglia Region; the wine is 75% Uva di Troia, 25% Montepulciano/Sangiovese and others, ruby-red with orange tints as it ages, dry, full-bodied, slightly tannic when young; a *riserva* is available.

ROSSO CONERO

(ROHS-soh koh-NAIR-oh)   **DOC**   Good red wine, much, but not all, made by the *governo* method (see), from 85% Montepulciano and 15% Sangiovese grapes, near Ancona, Marche Region, dry, robust, to be drunk young or before its fifth birthday, except for the best vintages. Conero is a Greek word for cherry — for the cherry trees covering the lower slopes of Mt. Conero; the wine is also known locally as Monte Conero. Let it breathe for two or three hours. Annual production is over two million liters. There is a good Moscato del Conero in the area but not yet a DOC.

ROSSO CORLEO

(ROHS-soh kohr-LAY-or)   Good red wine made in Sicily Region from Pignatello/Frappato/Nerello grapes.

ROSSO DAI VIGNETTI

(ROHS-soh day veen-AY-tee)   A red wine from young Brunello vines in the Brunello Di Montalcino area (see) of Tuscany Region; the grapes do not have the characteristics required for the greater wine, so they are fermented and the wine is bottled under the lesser name.

ROSSO DEL MOLISE

(ROHS-soh del mo-LEE-sa)   Dry red wine made mostly from the Sangiovese grape all over the Molise Region. This, with a Bianco Del Molise, are candidates for DOC.

ROSSO DELLE COLLINE LUCCHESI

(ROHS-soh del-la kohl-LEE-na look-KAY-see)   **DOC**   Good red wine made in the hills N of Lucca in Tuscany Region; similar to a Chianti but lighter; from 45-60% Sangiovese, 8-15% Canaiolo, 5-15% Ciliegiolo, 10-15% Trebbiano, 5-10% Malvasia/Vermentino grapes; best when young and can vary considerably as one can see from the allowable percentages.

ROSSO DI CERIGNOLA

(ROHS-soh dee chay-reen-YOH-la)   **DOC**   A red wine from the town of Cerignola, SE of Foggia, Puglia Region; made from 55% Uva Di Troia, 15% Negroamara and a maximum of 15% Sangiovese/Barbera/Montepulciano/ Malbec/Trebbiano and other grapes (!); it develops a brick-red tint with age which it needs; dry, full-bodied, slightly bitter after-taste; a *riserva* with two years in the wood, peaks about five.

ROSSO DI CILENTO

(ROHS-soh dee chee-LAYN-toh)   A good red, dry, strong, *spumante* made S of Salerno in Campania Region.

ROSSO DI SAVA

(ROHS-so dee SAH-va)   Good red wine from Primitivo grapes made near Taranto, Puglia Region, dry, full-bodied, often quite strong.

ROSSO PICENO

(ROHS-soh pee-CHAY-noh)   **DOC**   Good red wine from 60% Sangiovese, 40% Montepulciano with some Trebbiano allowed; made in much of the E and S parts of the Marche Region; dry, well-balanced, full-bodied, needs a little age but drink it before five; a *superiore* is available; needs 2-3 hours to breathe; about ten million liters made annually. A good white wine is made here in this general area but not yet DOC.

ROUCHET

(roo-SHAYT)   Superior red wine grape grown to a very limited extent in the Monferrato Hills, Piedmont Region; it produces a superior wine, deep ruby-red tending to violet, dry, robust, yet smooth with a few years of age. Very limited production and hard to find but worth it!!

ROUSANNE

(roo-SAHN-na)   Excellent white wine grape grown near Lucca in Tuscany Region.

RUBESCO

(roo-BAYS-koh)   A brand name for a Torgiana wine (see) made in Umbria Region.

RUBINO

(roo-BEE-noh)   The color "ruby" — in Italian.

RUBINO DI CANTAVENNA

(roo-BEE-noh dee kahn-ta-VAYN-na)   **DOC**   From a tiny area S of Asti in Piedmont Region, made from 75-95% Barbera and up to 25% Grignolino/ Freisa grapes; a good dry, light red, medium-bodied wine which improves with a little age.

RUFINA

(roo-FEE-na)   One of the seven zones of Chianti (see); produces an elegant wine.

RULANDER

The name used in German-speaking areas for the Pinot Grigio (Pinot Gris) grape. See Alto Adige.

S

SACRANTINO – SACRAMENTINO – SAGRANTINO
See Montefalco.

SALENTO PENINSULA
(sah-LAYN-toh) The "heel of the boot" – extending into the Adriatic Sea and forming the E landfall for the Gulf of Taranto, Puglia Region.

SALERNO
(sah-LAIR-noh) City of 50,000 on the Gulf of Salerno, S of the Bay of Naples, Campania Region – a tourist must!

SALICE SALENTINO
(SAH-lee-chay sah-layn-TEE-noh) **DOC** Salice is a small town about 10 miles W of Lecce on the Salento Peninsula, Puglia Region; the wine is made from 80% Negroamaro and 20% Red Malvasia grapes; dark red tending to orange with age (it needs a little); dry, robust, full-bodied, yet smooth; a *riserva* is available, also a rosé.

SALINA
(sah-LEE-nah) One of the Liparian Islands off the NE tip of Sicily Region, source of some of the best Malvasia Di Lipari.

SAMBIASE
(sahm-bee-AH-say) Small village near Catanzaro, Calabria Region, and a strong red wine made there.

SAN BARBATO
(sahn bar-BAH-toh) Red, white and rosé wines made in Gambatesa near Campobasso in Molise Region; one of the first of the wines to be bottled, labeled and exported presaging a trend in this Region to more prestigious wines with DOC status; the *bianco* is made from Trebbiano and Bombino grapes; the *rosato* and *rosso* are from Montepulciano and Sangiovese grapes.

SAN GIMIGNANO

See Vernaccia Di San Gimignano.

SAN MARINO

(sahn mah-REE-no) Small independent "postage stamp" Republic in the SE corner of Emilia-Romagna Region; it is the oldest republic, dating from the 4th Century, still in existence; about 20 square miles in area and 2000 feet above the beautiful beaches of Rimini.

SAN SEVERO

(sahn say-VAY-roh) **DOC** A small town in the N end of Puglia Region, producing three good wines for an annual production of three million liters — made here since 1300 AD.

BIANCO

(bee-AHN-koh) is from 40-60% Bombino, 40-60% Trebbiano, to 20% Malvasia/Verdeca grapes; straw-colored, dry fresh, carafe wine, better with a little age; a *spumante* is made.

ROSATO

(roh-SAH-toh) is from 70-100% Montepulciano and 30% Sangiovese grapes; typical rosé color, dry, drink it young.

ROSSO

(ROHS-soh) is also made from 70-100% Montepulciano and 30% Sangiovese grapes for a deep ruby-red, dry, medium-bodied wine needing a little age for smoothness.

SAN SIDERO

(sahn see-DAIR-oh) Red wine made from the Maglioppo grape in the Calabria Region.

SAN TORPE

(sahn TOR-pay) See Bianco Pisane Di San Torpe.

SANGIOVESE

(sahn-joh-VAY-say) Superior red wine grape grown in most of the Regions S of the Po River; it is probably the best red wine grape after the Nebbiolo; the informing grape in Chianti and other fine red wines; it generally needs age to soften the tannin. Some producers are experimenting with combining Cabernet Sauvignon and Merlot with it for some interesting results.

SANGIOVESE DEI COLLI PESARESI

(sahn-joh-VAY-say day KOHL-lee pay-sahr-AY-see) **DOC** A dry red wine of 85% Sangiovese and 15% Montepulciano/Ciliegiolo grapes, made in the Pesaro Hills in the E corner of Marche Region; slightly bitter after-taste, needs three to five years of age; let it breathe two to three hours upon opening.

SANGIOVESE DEL RUBICONE

(sahn-joh-VAY-say del roo-bee-KOHN-a) A good red wine from this grape from this river valley in the Emilia-Romagna Region.

SANGIOVESE DI APRILIA

(sahn-joh-VAY-say dee ah-PREE-lee-ah) **DOC** Aprilia is the new wine area S of Rome in Lazio Region; the Sangiovese grape seems to produce here a wine a little lighter than those farther north; it is its usual ruby-red, tannic when young, dry, good with three years of age.

SANGIOVESE DI ROMAGNA

(sohn-joh-VAY-say dee roh-MAHN-ya) **DOC** From the Emilia-Romagna Region, this is the "old stand-by" and an excellent taste reference; ruby-red with orange tints as it ages, dry, slightly bitter after-taste; a *superiore* is available; a *riserva* with two years of age, really needs three and much better with five; at least 40 million liters made annually.

SANGUE DI GIUDA

(SAHN-gay dee JOO-dah) **DOC** A very good dry, red wine from Barbera/Croatina/Ughetta/Uva Rara grapes, sturdy and full-bodied. The name is translated "Blood of Judas" and it is part of the Oltrepò Pavese, Lombardy Region.

SANT'ANNA DI ISOLA CAPO RIZZUTO

(sahn-TAHN-na dee ee-SOH-la KAH-poh reetz-TZOO-toh) **DOC** A good dry wine — the name is much bigger than the wine — from 40-60% Gaglioppo, 40-60% Nocera/Greco and other grapes, made on the Ionian coast just S of Crotone; a *rosato* is also produced here.

SANTA CHIARA

(SAHN-ta key-AHR-ah)   Brand name of an excellent red wine from the Nebbiolo grape with possibly some Bonarda, named for the monastery in Gattinara, Piedmont Region.

SANTA GIUSTINA

(SAHN-ta joo-STEE-na)   **LEITACHER**   Excellent red wine from the Schiava grape made N of Bolzano in the Trentino-Alto Adige Region; dry, medium-bodied, a little lighter than the famous Santa Maddelena from the same Region.

SANTA MADDELENA

(SAHN-ta mahd-day-LAY-na)   **SANKT MAGDALENER, DOC**   A superior red wine, one of Italy's best and famous for many years, made N and E of Bolzano in the Trentino-Alto Adige Region entirely from Schiava grapes; it is big, fruity, well-rounded with two years of age; there is a *classico* zone; some tasters detect a violet scent.

SANTA MARIA DELLA VERSA

(SAHN-ta mah-REE-ah del-la VAIR-sa)   The Versa valley near Pavia in Lombardy Region produces many excellent white wines from Chardonnay, Moscato and Riesling grapes; also much good *spumante* from various grapes.

SANTO STEFANO

(SAHN-toh stay-FAH-no)   Red wine made from the Montepulciano/Troia/ Barbera grapes in the town of Cerignola, Puglia Region; a big red wine needing age to soften.

SARDEGNA

(SAHR-DAYN-ya) or Sardinia — as we know it. An island Region of 9302 square miles, 1½ million people, Capitol city is Cagliari, a port on the S coast. An interesting story of its origin is: God, after finishing Earth, had a handful left over, so He dropped it, put His foot on it, and called it Sardinia! It does have many miles of spectacularly beautiful coast line and one can easily see why it has become an expatriate paradise for many Europeans and Americans since WWII. It was first settled by the Carthaginians, conquered

by Rome in 238 BC, then the Vandals, the Byzantine Empire, claimed by the Pope, the Arabs fought for it from the 8th to the 11th Centuries; Pisa and Genoa fought many battles for its sovereignty. Finally in the 14th Century, the Pope gave it to Spain, later to Austria, then Spain seized it, and it was finally awarded to the Duke of Savoy (the ruler of Piedmont) in exchange for his claim to Sicily. The Duke took his title as King of Sardinia; a later ruler, Victor Emmanuel II, and Count Cavour, his Prime Minister, were very instrumental in fomenting and completing the Risorgimento (with Garibaldi), in 1870 when Italy was finally declared free and unified. The United States was instrumental in providing control of the severe malarial problem which had always plagued the island, shortly after WW II. It is an important source for cork, as the tree, the cork oak, grows all over the island. For many years its wines were traditionally strong, robust — "separating the men from the boys" type, but much has been done in the last ten years to make them more in tune with the times. The most prolific vines — Cannonau, Monica, Giro and Torbato are thought to have come from Spain. The annual wine production is over 200 million liters.

COSTA SMERALDA

SORSO

ALGHERO

BOSA   NUORO

DORGALI

ORISTANO

CAGLIARI

SULCIS   **SARDINIA REGION**

SARTICOLA

(sahr-TEE-koh-la)   A golden, rich, sweet dessert wine made in Liguria Region, from *passito* grapes of many kinds.

SASSARI

(SAHS-sar-ee)   Small town in Sardinia Region, important as a production center for cork and Vermentino di Gallura (see).

SASSELLA

(sahs-SEL-lah)   One of the best of the red wines made in the Valtellina area of Lombardy Region from the Nebbiolo grape; very well-balanced, dry, medium-bodied, better with a little age. Sassella is a town in the area. See Valtellina Superiore.

SASSICAIA

(sahs-see-KAH-ya)   Superb red wine from Cabernet Sauvignon grapes made at Bolghieri S of Livorno in Tuscany Region — a brand name. This is the wine that stood the "wine world" on its head by taking an unprecedented perfect score from two tasters at the now-famous Decanter Magazine tasting in London in 1978 — and is an example of the superior wines that Italy can produce from this grape; it is hard to find in this country at the moment because of the extremely limited production.

SAUVIGNON

(so-veen-YONH)   or Sauvignon Blanc as it is most often called in America. A superior white wine grape grown in the Trentino-Alto Adige, Veneto and Friuli Regions — probably brought from France; it produces excellent wines in these Regions, frequently a little lighter than in France and California.

SAVINELLO

(sah-veen-EL-lo)   Good red wine from Sangiovese and Ciliegiolo grapes made near Chieti in Abruzzo Region; ruby-red, fresh, dry, medium-bodied, slight almond taste; a *rosato* is also made. Candidate for DOC.

SAVOY   —   HOUSE OF SAVOY

A dynasty dating to the 11th Century ruling parts of France, Switzerland and Italy, titular rulers of the Kingdoms of Jerusalem, Cyprus and Armenia, actually ruling Piedmont and other areas as Kings of Sardinia; chosen as Kings of Italy at the end of the Risorgimento, and ruled until abdication in 1946.

SAVUTO

(sah-VOO-toh)   **DOC**   Wine made in the central part of Calabria Region since ancient times; both *rosato* and *rosso* are made from 35-45% Gaglioppo, 30-40% Greco Nero, to 10% Sangiovese, to 25% Malvasia Bianco/Pecorino grapes; the color and taste will vary with this tolerance in grapes; on the whole it is dry, full-bodied and needs a little age; a *superiore* is available.

SCACCIADIAVOLI

(skah-chah-dee-AH-voh-lee)   Red wine made from Barbera and Montepulciano grapes in Umbria Region; ruby-red, tannic, dry and strong; it has an interesting translation — "chase the devils away."

SCANDIANO

(skahn-dee-AH-no)   Good white wine grape grown in Emilia-Romagna Region and the wine from it — straw-colored, dry, fresh carafe wine; a sweet *spumante* made also.

SCELTO

(SHAYL-toh)   Selected — the process of selecting grapes individually for perfection.

SCHIAVA

(skee-AH-va)   Superior red wine grape grown in northern Italy, mostly in the Trentino-Alto Adige Region where the German name is VERNATSCH. The wine is often light in body with much rosé made in the Region from it.

SCHIACCHETRA

See Cinqueterre.

SCHIOPPETTINO

(sheeoh-pet-TEE-no)   An unusual red wine from Ribolla grapes made N of Udine in the Friuli-Venezia Giulia Region; dark red with violet shading, dry, tannic, robust; an excellent wine but hard to find.

SCIASCINOSSO

(shah-shee-NOHS-so)   Red wine grape grown in Campania Region.

SECCO

(SAYK-koh)   Dry. The progression of sweetness in Italian wines:

secco — less than 1%;   abboccato — 1-2%;
amabile — 2½-3%;   dolce — 3-6% sugar.

SEGESTA

(say-JES-tah)   (1)   Ancient Greek city in ruins, near Alcamo W of Palmero, Sicily Region;   (2)   Red and white wines made there today, light-bodied, semi-dry.

SELE

(SAY-lay)   River in Campania Region rising near the border of Basilicata Region, flowing N then W to the Gulf of Salerno. Good red and white wines in the entire valley.

SEMIDANO

(say-mee-DAHN-oh)   Good white wine grape grown in the Sardinia Region.

SEMILLION

(say-mee-YONH)   Excellent white wine grape from France; grown to a limited extent in Trentino-Alto Adige Region.

SERPRINA

(sayr-PREE-nah)   Ordinary white wine grape grown in Veneto Region; see Colli Euganei.

SETTESOLI

(sayt-tay-SOH-lee)   Good wines made near Menfi in the SW part of Sicily Region; the *bianco* is from Trebbiano/Inzolia and is light and dry; the *rosato* and *rosso* are made from Nero D'Avola/Pignatello grapes; both light and dry; the red is probably the best of the three.

SFORZATO or **SFURSAT**

(sfohr-TZAH-toh / sfohr-SAHT)   See Valtellina.

SIBIOLA

(see-bee-OH-la)   Brand name for excellent red and rosé wines made from 40% Cannonau, 40% Monica and 20% Barbera grapes, NE of Cagliari, Sardinia Region.

SICILIA

(see-CHEE-lee-ah)   We spell it Sicily — named for the ancient tribe Siculi; the largest island in the Mediterranean Sea, called Trinacria by the ancients; settled by the Greeks, Carthaginians and Phoenicians all about the same time — 8th Century BC (give or take a century); conquered by Rome (it was their granary), then by the Goths, in the 9th Century by the Arabs, then the Normans, the Swabians, then claimed by the Pope who gave it to the French, then Spain, then in 1713 to the House of Savoy, who exchanged it in 1720 for a clear title to Sardinia. Spain then ruled it as part of the Kingdom of Naples and later the Kingdom of The Two Sicilies until it was over-run by Garibaldi in 1860 as the first conflict of the Risorgimento.

The Region is 9930 square miles in area, above five million in population, the Capitol city is Palermo — a fine harbor on the N coast; home of the Mafia, Marsala and Mt. Etna — an active volcano on the E Coast. Sicilian wines for centuries were "rough and ready" — hardly saleable or even palatable to other than Sicilians. There are many co-ops doing an excellent job with wines and, since 1970 especially, great strides have been made to improve the quality and saleability with almost spectacular results. The average annual production has fallen somewhat below the one billion liter mark.

SICILY REGION

SIENA

(see-AY-nah) City of about 50,000 people in central Tuscany Region famous in history from the beginning, in the Medieval period and later; magnificent art and architecture abounds, etc. The area between it and Florence is the famous *classico* zone of Chianti (see); it is also the location of a fine *enoteca* officially the national wine museum, located in a former Medici fortress.

SIFONE

(see-FOH-nay) Sweetened, thickened grape juice used in making Marsala (see).

SIRICUSA

(seer-ee-KOO-sa) A city of 118,000 people founded by the Greeks and the center of their culture on the island of Sicily until sacked by Rome in 212 BC and declined thereafter. Pliny the Elder, who loved Sicily, wrote of the wine of the time — Siracusanum — a favorite of Rome.

SIZZANO

(seetz-TZAH-no) **DOC** Excellent red wine from 40-60% Nebbiolo, 15-40% Vespolina, and a maximum of 25% Bonarda grapes, made in the Novara Hills of the Piedmont Region; dry, rich, full-bodied, it must have three years of age (two in wood) before release; much better with ten years behind it — about 125,000 liters produced annually.

SOAVE

(soh-AH-vay) **DOC** Another of the excellent Italian wines known around the world — made since 1300 in Soave, a beautiful small town dominated by a crenellated castle, near Verona in the E part of the Veneto Region. The wine is made from 70-90% Garganega and 10-30% Trebbiano grapes, clear with a slight greenish tint, dry, medium-bodied, well-rounded, a wine to serve with that special luncheon. There is a *classico* zone, a *superiore*, and some *spumante* made, also a Recioto Di Soave (see). Avoid if it is over four years old; serve just lightly chilled. Annual production is about 50 million liters.

SOGNO DI BACCO

SOHN-yo dee BAHK-ko) A superior red wine (brand name) made of Nebbiolo/Bonarda/Vespolina grapes in Gattinara, Piedmont Region; dry, full-bodied, long-lived, aged five years before release; hard to find, but worth it. The name is translated "Bacchus dream."

SOLIMANO

(soh-lee-MAHN-no)   A brand name for rich, sweet dessert wine made from the Zibibbo grape on the island of Pantelleria, Sicily Region.

SOLOPACA

(SOH-loh-pah-kah)   **DOC**   This small town is about 40-odd miles N of Caserta, Campania Region; and produces:

BIANCO

(bee-AHN-koh)   from 50-70% Trebbiano with two kinds of Malvasia grapes; dry, smooth, better with a little age and lightly chilled.

ROSSO

(ROHS-soh)   is from 45-50% Sangiovese, 10-20% Aglianico, 20-25% Piedi-rosso and to 10% Sciascinoso; ruby-red, dry, medium-bodied, needs a little age to be smooth.

SOLUNTO

(soh-LOON-toh)   Brand name for very good red, white and rosé wines made near Palermo in Sicily Region.

SONDRIO

(SOHN-dree-oh)   Town along the Adda River in the Valtellina area of Lombardy Region; center of that wine trade.

SORNI

(SOHR-nee   **DOC**   A village N of Trento in the Trentino-Alto Adige Region producing very good wines that were mostly exported to Germany and Switzerland for many years.

BIANCO

(bee-AHN-koh)   is from 70% Nosiola and 30% Muller-Thurgau; straw-colored, medium-dry, fresh-tasting, a good carafe wine.

ROSSO

(ROHS-so)   is made from 70% Schiava, 20-30% Teroldego and 10% Lagrein for a ruby-red, medium-bodied, dry, smooth wine.

SPANNA

(SPAHN-na)   The local name in part of the Piedmont area for the famous Nebbiolo grape, often labeled as such; the wine is lighter than the Barolo, but with three to five years of age, it is rich, smooth, full-bodied, dry, and red, of course! Often a better wine than many others made from the Nebbiolo grape and generally a good buy; peaks about 6 to 8 years.

SPOLETO

(spoh-LAY-toh)   Old city in the Umbria Region, important in the Etruscan era; the seat of the Duchy of Spoleto which included much of Umbria, Marche and Abruzzo Regions — later part of the Papal States (see).

SPUMANTE

(spoo-MAHN-tay)   Italian for sparkling; every Region makes some sparkling wines; they are great favorites in Italy.

SPUMANTE BRUT

(spoo-MAHN-tay BROOT)   This sparking white wine is made from the white Pinot grapes (and some Pinot Nero) but definitely not the Moscato grape of Asti Spumante — one of two major differences; the second is that it is made in the bottle, the *metodo champenois* which originated in France; it is dry, fruity, aged for three years and the vintage must be shown on the label; about 100 million liters produced annually in the Veneto, Friuli-Venezia Giulia and Trentino-Alto Adige Regions, with some of the finest made in the Trento area.

SQUINZANO

(skween-TZAH-noh) **DOC** A small town S of Brindisi in the Salento Peninsula of Puglia Region; there is no *bianco* in the DOC.

ROSATO

(roh-SAH-toh) is made from 55% or more Negroamaro, 30% Red Malvasia, to 15% Sangiovese grapes; typical rosé color light-bodied, dry.

ROSSO

(ROHS-soh) is made from 55% or more Negroamaro, a maximum of 30% Red Malvasia and 15% Sangiovese grapes; a deep ruby-red with orange tints as it ages, dry and full-bodied; a *riserva* is available.

STERI

(STAIR-ee) Brand name for a good red wine made from Barbera and one of the Lambrusco vines (yes) in the SW part of Sicily Region; an unusual ruby-red, semi-dry wine.

STRAVECCHIO

(strah-VAYK-kee-oh) Very old.

STROMBOLI

(STROM-boh-lee) One of the Liparian Islands off the NE tip of Sicily with an active, constantly erupting volcano.

SUDTIROL

The German name for the South Tyrol, or Alto Adige area of the Trentino-Alto Adige Region; often seen on wine labels in this bi-lingual Region.

SUGAR

is not allowed in Italian wines — under the EEC rules; where the word is used in this volume, it refers to sweetness, rather than the actual use of sugar as the layman might well presume. (It is also prohibited in California.)

SUPERIORE

(soo-pay-ree-OR-ay) Superior. No legal meaning on a wine label, unless it is a DOC wine; then it is defined for each wine — usually slightly older with a slightly greater alcoholic content.

SYBARIS

An ancient Greek colony founded about 1000 BC on the Gulf of Taranto; supposedly a city where vice REALLY flourished!

SYLVANER

(sil-VAHN-air) The white wine grape transported to Italy and grown to a limited extent in the northern Regions; see Alto Adige and Terlano.

T

TAGLIO

(TAHL-yo) A wine of high alcoholic content, or strong color, or strong body, used to give its properties to a lesser wine — a most proper part of the art of blending wines. Prior to the 1970s many of the wines made in southern Italy were of this type.

TANIT

(TAH-neet) A brand name for a strong, sweet, rich wine made from the Zibibbo grape, typical Muscat aroma and flavor, from the island of Pantelleria. Tanit was a goddess in Greek mythology.

TAORMINA

(tah-or-MEEN-ah) A beautiful resort town and area at the foot of Mt. Etna on the E coast of Sicily Region; the wines made there today are mostly white, dry and fresh-tasting, from Catarratto/Carricante/Inzolia grapes.

TAURASI

(taw-RAH-see) **DOC** Superior red wine made from 70-100% Aglianico, or with to 30% Piedirosso/Sangiovese/Barbera grapes, near Avellino, Campania Region; deep ruby-red, dry, robust, full-bodied, must have three years of age before release; a *riserva* with four years, better with five or ten!! One of Italy's best reds that will live and improve for much longer.

TEGOLATO

(tay-go-LAH-toh) A brand name for a superior Chianti from Tuscany Region; the name comes from the tiled roof as the wine is kept in the attic and works or sleeps with the temperature; this reduces the time spent in aging.

TENEMENTI

(tay-nay-MEN-tee)   An estate producing wine.

TENUTA   VINICOLA

(tay-NOO-tah VEE-nee-koh-la)   A vineyard and winery operation — an area where all the operations are performed.

TERLANER

(tair-LAH-nair)   German name for the wines produced in Terlano, which was formerly known as Terlan; the Region is Trentino-Alto Adige.

TERLANO

(tair-LAH-noh)   **TERLANER DOC**   The town of Terlano is N of Bolzano, Trentino-Alto Adige Region and has been famous for its wines for many years — and particularly a white by this name. With the exception of that one wine, they are labeled with the variety of the grape used and must be 90% of that variety. There are no red wines in this DOC zone.

TERLANO

(tair-LAH-no)   is made from 50% Pinot Bianco with the other 50% from Riesling Italico/Riesling Renano/Sauvignon/Sylvaner grapes; even with these tolerances, this is an excellent carafe wine, made for quaffing — semi-dry and well-balanced in all respects.

PINOT   BIANCO

(Pee-no bee-AHN-ko)   is an excellent example of this variety, dry and medium-bodied.

RIESLING   ITALICO

(REES-ling ee-TAHL-ee-ko)   is dry, medium-bodied, excellent as an aperitif.

RIESLING   RENANO

(REES-ling ray-NAH-no)   Dry, good body, fruity — overall an excellent wine — better, as a rule, than the Italico.

SAUVIGNON

(sew-veen-YONH)   is a very good, dry, medium-bodied wine with good flavor.

SYLVANER

(sil-VAH-nair)   is softer than the other wines, semi-dry almost *amabile* but a good wine for those who like their wines sweeter.

MULLER   —   THURGAU

(MOO-lair TOOR-gow)   semi-dry, medium-bodied, similar to the Sylvaner.

TERMENO

(tair-MAY-no)   Village near Lake Caldaro called Tramin under the Austrians; supposedly the home of the Traminer grape; the Region is the Trentino-Alto Adige.

TERNI

(TAIR-nee)   Small town near Orvieto, Umbria Region, where much Orvieto is made.

TEROLDEGO ROTALIANO

(tair-ohl-DAY-go roh-TAHL-ee-AHN-oh) **DOC** Excellent wine made from 90% Teroldego, 10% Lagrein/Pinot Nero grapes; deep ruby-red, big, strong, dry, tannic when young, but full-bodied and smooth when aged; peaks at about four years; a *riserva* is available; in good years, this can be a tremendous wine. Rotaliano is a plain N of Trento at the junction of the Noce (NOH-chay) and Adige Rivers, the Trentino-Alto Adige Region.

TERRALBA

See Campidano Di Terralba.

TERRANO DEL CARSO

(tair-RAH-noh del KAR-so) Red wine from the Refosco grape made near Trieste in the Friuli-Venezia Giulia Region; purple-red, rough, sometimes *frizzante*; to be drunk in its first year.

TEVERE RIVER — TIBER RIVER

Rises in Tuscany Region and flows mostly south through Umbria Region, turning W at Todi on its way through Lazio Region to empty into the Tyrrhenian Sea, for a total length of about 240 miles.

TICINO RIVER

Rises in Switzerland and flows through Lake Maggiore, then forming part of the boundary between Piedmont and Lombardy Regions, emptying into the Po River south of Pavia.

TIGNANELLO

(teen-ya-NEL-loh) The brand name for a superior red wine made in Tuscany Region from Sangiovese and the other Chianti grapes, but with about 10% Cabernet Sauvignon grapes added; deep-red, dry, rich, full-bodied, fragrant and made only in the best years; let it breathe for four hours, and it may need decanting.

TINTIGLIA

(teen-TEE-lee-yah)   Ordinary red, slightly sweet wine made from the Tintore grape on the island of Ischia in the Bay of Naples, Campania Region.

TINTORE

(teen-TOHR-ay)   Red wine grape grown on the island of Ischia and the wine from it — Campania Region.

TOCAI or **TOCAI FRIULANO**

(toh-KIE free-oo-LAHN-oh)   Superior white wine grape grown heavily in Friuli-Venezia Giulia which is its home; in Veneto (Tocai Di Lison, Vini Del Piave, Colli Berici) and to a lesser extent in Lombardy near Lake Garda with minor amounts grown in Emilia-Romagna and Umbria Regions. It is the most popular white wine in its home Region (F-VG) with about 8 million liters made annually; it produces a dry, crisp, medium-bodied wine just right for "quaffing" anytime, and the closest to an everyday wine if the Friulians have one. One story says it originated in Hungary (although there is no connection to the Hungarian Tokaji) and another story says it went from Italy to Hungary (who claimed it as her own) and then returned to Friuli! There is also a red variety grown to a small extent.

TOCAI DEL PIAVE

See Vini Del Piave.

TOCAI DI LISON

(toh-KIE dee lee-SOHN)   **DOC**   Lison is a small town in Veneto Region where much wine is made from this grape; it is not as good as in Friuli as a general rule; straw-colored, dry, good body, slightly bitter after-taste; good with fish; a *classico* is available. There is a new DOC zone proposed to cover this area. See Lison-Pramaggiore.

TOCAI DI SAN MARTINO DELLA BATTAGLIA

(toh-KIE dee sahn mar-TEE-no del-la baht-TAHL-ya)   **DOC**   A long name to make a simple wine carry! The area is S of Lake Garda in Lombardy Region; the grape is the Tocai — the wine is pale yellow, dry, light and fresh; drink before it is three; good with fish.

TODI

(TOH-dee)   Town on the Tiber River in Umbria Region where it turns W toward Lazio. See Greco Di Todi.

TORBATO

(tohr-BAH-toh)   Good white wine grape believed to have come from Spain to the Sardinia Region; the wine from it is straw-colored with green tints, dry, well-balanced, medium-bodied; there is also a *passito* made — Torbato Passito.

TORCOLATO

(tohr-koh-LAH-to)   Dessert wine from Tocai, Vespaiolo and Garganega grapes, *passito*, in the Breganze area of Veneto Region.

TORGIANO

(tohr-jee-AH-no)   **DOC**   The small town of Torgiano is S of Perugia on the Tiber River in Umbria Region; two wines have been made there for hundreds of years — over 1½ million liters made every year.

BIANCO

(bee-AHN-koh)   is made from 50-70% Trebbiano, 15-35% Grechetto, to 15% Malvasia/Verdello; straw-colored, dry, fruity and sharp when young, much better with a few years of age. That exported to this country is a brand labeled: Torre Di Giano; the *rosso* is labeled Rubesco.

ROSSO

(ROHS-soh)   is made from 50-70% Sangiovese, 15-30% Canaiolo, 10% Trebbiano, 10% Montepulciano/Ciliegiolo grapes; it has a distinctive flavor, dry, full-bodied, needs six to eight years of age when it is suddenly smooth and well-rounded; a *riserva* is available.

TORINO

(tohr-EE-no)   We spell it Turin — the Capitol of Piedmont Region, city of 2 million people, seat of the Savoy monarchy for centuries — and a magnificent palace and much fine classical architecture; there is a fine automobile museum and this city is not only the center of the Vermouth trade but also the birthplace of breadsticks. The university was founded in the 15th Century.

TORRE ALEMANNA

(tohr-RAY ahl-ay-MAHN-na)   Good red wine made in Puglia Region.

TORRE DEI PASSERI

(tohr-RAY day PAHS-say-ree)   Good red wine made from Montepulciano grapes in this town SW of Pescara in the Abruzzo Region.

TORRE DI GIANO

(tohr-RAY dee jee-AHN-oh)   A brand name of Torgiano exported to America. See Torgiano above.

TORRE ERCOLANA

(tohr-RAY air-koh-LAH-na)   Brand name for a superior red wine made from Cabernet Sauvignon, Cesanese and Merlot grapes in Rome, Lazio Region, included here for its unusual formula; it is rich, dry, full-bodied; the production is small and it is hard to find outside of Rome.

 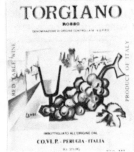 

TORRE QUARTO

(tohr-ray KAR-toh)   Brand name for excellent red and white wines made near Foggia in Puglia Region; the red is a superior wine.

BIANCO
(bee-AHN-koh)   is from Bombino/Trebbiano grapes, and perhaps others; dry, full-bodied for a white but drink it before its third birthday.

ROSSO
(ROHS-soh)   is made from Barbera/Sangiovese/Malbec/Aglianico grapes; quite complex, robust, full-bodied, dry; it needs at least five years of age to be smooth and improves until it is ten. A *rosato* is also made.

TORRELSALSA

(tohr-ray-SAHL-sa)   Brand name for very good red, white and rosé wines made near Agrigento in Sicily Region; the *bianco* is from Trebbiano/Catarratto/Inzolia grapes; the *rosato* and *rosso* are made from Vernaccia/Frappato/Nerello grapes.

TORRETTE

(Fr: TOR-et)   A superior red wine from the Petit Rouge grape and made in the Aosta Valley (and Region); a light body and flavor that intensifies with age for many years. Torrette is the name of a zone — candidate for DOC to include the following wines:

Vin de la Colline d'Aosta,

Vin de Sarre-Chesallet   —   Vin Torrette de St. Pierre

Vin de Villeneuve   — Vin de l'Envers.

TOSCANA

(toh-SKAH-na)   or Tuscany as we spell it — a Region of 8876 square miles in area, three million plus in population, the N central part of Italy; bounded on the N and E by Liguria and Emilia-Romagna Regions, on the S by Umbria and Lazio Regions and on the W by the Tyrrhenian Sea; its Capitol is Florence and its chief port is Livorno (Leghorn); rich in history, home of the Etruscan civilization, conquered by the Romans in the third century BC; a Duchy under the Lombard Kingdom and much internal fighting among the cities and families for the next hundreds of years; after the Medici family died, it became the prize of European thrones (and wars) until annexed by the Kingdom of Sardinia early in the Risorgimento. Its cities are rich in art and architecture, the Arno River drains much of the N plain before emptying into the Tyrrhenian Sea near Pisa; Elba was the exiled home of Napoleon, etc., etc. The average annual wine production is 450 million liters, with the best known probably Chianti.

TUSCANY REGION

TRAMINER OR TRAMINER AROMATICO

(trah-MEEN-air)   Excellent white wine grape grown in northern Italy; its origin is supposedly the village of Tramin (under the Austrians), now known as Termeno, near Lake Caldaro in the Trentino-Alto Adige Region. The wine it produces is generally light, fresh, and dry, with a distinct aroma and spiciness. The grape is often called the Gewurztraminer elsewhere.

TRAMONTI

(trah-MOHN-tee)   Red wine made near Salerno, Campania Region, from Coda Di Volpe/Tintore/Strepparosa grapes, ruby-red, light-bodied, slightly sweet.

TREBBIANINO VAL TREBBIA

(trayb-bee-an-NEE-no vahl TRAYB-bee-ah)   **DOC**   The Trebbia valley is S of Picenza in the NW tip of Emilia-Romagna Region; the wine is made from 35-50% Ortrugo, 10-30% Malvasia, 15-30% Trebbiano/Moscato and to 15% Sauvignon; a good carafe wine, it is aromatic and light-bodied, made both dry and sweet; drink it young.

TREBBIANO

(trayb-bee-AH-no)   The Trebbia Valley is S of Picenza in the NW tip of Emilia-Romagna and is supposedly the origin of this grape — an excellent white wine grape grown all over Italy S of the Po River; its big yield makes it a popular variety. It is so often mixed with Malvasia in varying quantities and should be drunk young, although it can hold its age alone.

TREBBIANO D'ABRUZZO

(trayb-bee-AH-no dah-BROOTZ-tzoh)   **DOC**   This wine is made all over the Abruzzo Region from the Trebbiano grape (85%), and about 15% of Malvasia; dry, medium-bodied, varies in taste among wineries, much improved in the last decade.

TREBBIANO DI APRILIA

(trayb-bee-AH-no dee ah-PREE-lee-ah)   **DOC**   White wine made from 95% Trebbiano grapes in the Aprilia area S of Rome, Lazio Region; deep yellow, almost gold, clear, dry, an excellent wine but drink it before it is three.

TRENTINO – ALTO ADIGE

(tren-TEE-no AHL-toh AH-dee-jay)   A land-locked Region of 5250 square miles in area, about one million population, the most northern part of Italy, very mountainous; bordered on the N by Austria, on the E and S by Veneto and on the W by Lombardy Regions; Trento is the Capitol. The Isarco River (see) drains the NE section, the Adige River drains the NW section and they meet at Bolzano on their way S and SE through Veneto to the Adriatic. This was all part of Austria for so many years and known as the South Tyrol; German and Italian are both official languages. The Brenner Pass has been the gateway from the N for invaders throughout the centuries; there are several good wine roads; the average annual wine production is over 150 million liters. See Alto Adige, Caldaro, Santa Maddalena, Terlano, Trentino and Valle Isarco for wines.

TRENTINO – ALTO ADIGE REGION

TRENTO

(TREN-toh)   City of 100,000 population, the Capitol of Trentino-Alto Adige Region; site of the famous Council of Trent in the 16th Century which revised the Catholic dogma over a period of 17 years; today an important wine center.

TRIESTE

(tree-ESS-tay)   City of 300,000 population and Italy's second port in importance (after Genoa) which was Austria's outlet to the sea under that occupation.

TROIA

(TROH-ya)   Red wine grape grown in Puglia Region; it produces a very rough red wine, a real *taglio* wine; the Puglians drink it young and fresh, but most of the Wine Drinkers of the World would probably shrink rather than drink!!

TURIN

See Torino.

TUSCAN WHITE

A catch-all generic term for the ordinary white carafe wine made all over Tuscany for centuries; much of it good — dry and semi-dry — from various mixtures of whatever was on hand, mostly Trebbiano and Malvasia. Prior to DOC, it was often called White Chianti but that name is now prohibited. There has been agitation to renew the name. See Bianco Della Lega and Galestro.

TUSCANY

See Toscana.

U

UDINE
(OO-dee-nay)   City of 60,000 people and Capitol of Friuli-Venezia Giulia Region. There was much damage N of the city in the destructive earthquake of 1976.

UMBRIA
(OOM-bree-ah)   A land-locked Region of 3281 square miles in area, about 800,000 population, bordered on the N by Tuscany, on the E by Marche and on the S and W by Lazio Region; the Capitol city is Perugia. This was Etruscan territory prior to the rise of the Roman Empire; after its fall, and various conquests, it became part of the Duchy of Spoleto until Papal authority became paramount in the 14th Century. There are many beautiful old cities — Assisi, Gubbio, Spoleto, Todi and Torgiano — two of the most beautiful cathedrals surviving the Medieval Ages are at Assisi and Orvieto. The Tiber River flows through the area from N to S into Lazio toward the sea. The average annual wine production is about 80 million liters with Orvieto probably the best-known. See also Colli Altotiberini, Colli Del Trasimeno, Montefalco and Torgiano for other wines.

UMBRIA REGION

UVA

(OO-va)   Grape. *Un grappolo d'uva* — a bunch of grapes; *pigiar l'uva* — to tread grapes.

UVA   DI   TROIA

(OO-va dee TRO-ya)   Red wine grape grown in Puglia Region and used in several of their wines.

UZZANO

(OOTZ-tzah-no)   A red wine made in the Tuscany Region.

V

V.I.D.E.

A new organization formed of producers in small to medium wineries, to promote and sell quality wines; a label with these letters will be affixed to the wines selected.

V.Q.P.R.D.

Loosely, an abbreviation of the title of the regulation of the European Common Market (ECM) for quality wines in specific regions. Included are the AOC wines of France, the DOC wines of Italy and the similar wines of Germany.

VAL

(VAHL)   Valley.

VAL DI PAGLIA

(VAHL dee PAHL-lee-ya)   Good white wine made near Orvieto in Umbria Region; dry, medium-body, sometimes *frizzante*. There is also a sweet red wine made near from the Aleatico grape — a *passito* type.

VAL VERSA

(vahl-VAIR-sa)   Several good white wines are made in this valley near Pavia in Lombardy Region from Cortese/Malvasia/Riesling grapes, also much good carafe wine.

VALCALEPIO

(vahl-kah-LAY-pee-oh)   **DOC**   Going NE from Milan towards Lago d'Iseo in the central part of Lombardy Region is a new zone making two excellent wines:

BIANCO

(bee-AHN-koh)   is from 55-75% Pinot Bianco and 25-45% Pinot Grigio grapes, straw-colored, dry and fresh.

ROSSO

(ROHS-soh)   is made from 55-75% Merlot and 25-45% Cabernet Sauvignon grapes; ruby-red, dry, full-bodied; must be aged for two years before release; peaks about six years.

VALDADIGE

(vahl-DAH-dee-jay)   Ger: **ETSCHALER   DOC**   These are the very good red and white wines that one finds all over the Adige Valley in the Trentino-Alto Adige Region:

BIANCO

(bee-AHN-koh)   is made from 20% each of Pinot Bianco/Pinot Grigio/Riesling Isalico/Muller-Thurgau and the balance of Bianchetta/Trebbiano/Nosiola/Vernaccia/Sylvaner/Veltliner!! One is amazed that this allowable group of grapes can always produce such a good carafe wine — made both dry and semi-dry and with a fresh, pleasant taste.

ROSSO

(ROHS-soh)   is from a minimum of 20% Schiava and 10% Lambrusco with the other 70% a mixture of Lagrein/Merlot/Negrara/Pinot Nero/Teroldego grapes; red, dry, a good "quaffing" wine not meant to age.

VALDICHIANA

(vahl-dee-key-AH-na)   The Chiana Valley S of Arezzo in Tuscany Region produces a great deal of white wine — probably from a Trebbiano base; generally dry, but is found semi-dry — fresh-tasting, drink it young.

VALDOBBIADENE

See Prosecco Di Conegliano-Valdobbiadene.

VALGELLA

(vahl-JEL-la)   Excellent red wine from the Nebbiolo grape named for this town in the Valtellina area of Lombardy Region; a little lighter than Barolo, but nonetheless a very good, dry, medium-bodied wine. See Valtellina Superiore.

VALLAGARINA

(vahl-lah-gar-EE-na)   Another of the good carafe wines from the Adige Valley of the Trentino-Alto Adige Region.

VALLE D'AOSTA

(VAHL DOHS-ta)   The smallest Region in Italy, land-locked, some 1260 square miles in area mostly of mountains, part of the Piedmont Region until after WWII; bordered on the N by Switzerland, on the E and S by Piedmont Region and on the W by France; its Capitol is Aosta in the Center of the Region; population is about 125,000 mostly French-speaking with both French and Italian as official languages; one can see the Matterhorn, Mont Blanc, Gran Paradiso, the two St. Bernard Passes to France and Switzerland, the Mont Blanc tunnel, much Roman architecture and a few examples of Medieval art. The average annual wine production is over three million liters, with Donnaz and Enfer D'Arviers their best-known wines; see also Blanc De Morgex, Chambave, Nus, Torrette and Vin d'Arnad.

1 — Mt. Blanc Tunnel
2 — Courmayer
3 — Morgex
4 — Aosta
5 — Nus
6 — Chatillon
7 — St. Vincent
8 — Dora Baltea R.
9 — Donnaz

VALLE D'AOSTA REGION

VALLE D'ITRIA

(VAHL-lay DEE-tree-ah)   Good red and white wines made in the Salento Peninsula, Puglia Region; Montepulciano and Sangiovese are the grapes in the red with Verdecca and others used in the white wine.

VALLE ISARCO

(VAHL-lay ee-SAHR-koh) **EISACKTALER DOC** This river drains the NE section of the Trentino-Alto Adige Region and joins the Adige River at Bolzano; many of the wines are exported to Germany and Switzerland, but some are found in America; they are varietally named and must be 90% of that variety. The labels often carry both the Italian and German in this bilingual Region. There are no red wines in this zone.

MULLER — THURGAU

(MOO-lair TOOR-gaw) is straw-colored, semi-dry, medium-bodied, a good carafe wine.

PINOT GRIGIO

(PEE-noh GREE-jee-oh) is white with a greenish tint, dry, medium-bodied, an excellent wine.

SYLVANER

(sil-VAHN-air) similar to the Muller-Thurgau, semi-dry, medium-bodied.

TRAMINER AROMATICO

(trah-MEEN-air ahr-oh-MAH-tee-koh) This is an excellent wine — spicy, fresh-tasting and dry.

VELTLINER

(VELT-lee-nair) is dry and fresh — a good carafe wine.

VALPANTENA

See Valpolicella.

VALPOLICELLA

(vahl-pol-ee-CHEL-la) **DOC** A superior red wine known around the world, made since the 16th century in this area — NW of Verona, Veneto Region; it is similar to the Bardolino in that it is made from the same grapes — 55-70% Corvina, 25-30% Rondinella, 5-15% Molinara and 10% others; dark red, dry, medium-bodied, much of it is made by the *governo* method; there is a *classico* zone and a *superiore* has an additional year of age; Valpantena may appear on the label if the grapes are from that valley; it is best to drink it under three years although it may last longer. Serve it with red meats, or a rich turkey. About 30 million liters produced annually. There is a Recioto Della Valpolicella (see) and an Amarone, the dry version of the Recioto; also a Kosher style made.

VALTELLINA

(vahl-tel-LEE-nah) **DOC** Very important wine area in the N part of Lombardy Region along the banks of the Adda River; the town of Sondrio is the center of this wine area; the informing grape is the Nebbiolo, locally called the Chiavennasca, at 70% with the other 30% of Pinot Nero/Merlot/Rossola/Brugnola/Pignola grapes allowed; dry, tannic when young, but with two years of age an excellent full-bodied red wine; about 4½ million liters made annually.

SFURSAT or SFORZATO

(sfor-SAHT or sfor-TZAHT-oh) is made with slightly-dried grapes, 15% alcohol, big, rich, usually dry but can be semi-dry — excellent with a fine beef roast.

VALTELLINA SUPERIORE

(vahl-tal-LEE-na soo-pay-ree-OHR-ay) **DOC** is produced in the towns of Grumello, Inferno, Sassella and Valgella, all in this same area; the Nebbiolo must be 95% and the wine is ruby-red, dry, full-bodied, but not quite up to the Barolo of Piedmont Region. The town names appear on the labels and many consider the Inferno to be the best; two years of age (one in wood) are required before release and with two more years, it may be a *riserva*; peaks about six years; production is over three million liters annually.

VECCHIO
(VAY-kee-oh)   Old.

VELLETRI
(vayl-LAY-tree)   **DOC**   Small town S of Rome, Lazio Region, the Castelli Romani area; there are two wines:

BIANCO
(bee-AHN-koh)   is from 60-70% Malvasia, a minimum of 30% Trebbiano and to 10% Bellone/Bonvino grapes; straw-colored, medium-bodied, made both *secco* and *amabile*.

ROSSO
(ROHS-soh)   is from 20-35% Sangiovese, 20-35% Montepulciano, a minimum of 30% Cesanese and 10% other grapes; ruby-red, dry, smooth, well-rounded with proper age; it is the only red wine in the Castelli Romani that is DOC.

VENDEMMIA
(ven-DAYM-mee-ah)   Vintage or harvest.

VENEGAZZÙ
(vay-nay-GAHTZ-tzoo)   Small town near Treviso, N of Venice in Veneto Region produces two superior wines.

BIANCO
(bee-AHN-koh)   is made from Pinot white and Riesling grapes; dry, fresh and pleasant.

ROSSO
(ROHS-soh)   is a red wine from Cabernet Sauvignon/Cabernet Franc/Merlot/Malbec/Petit Verdot grapes (shades of Bordeaux!); rich, dry, full-bodied, wonderful with proper age and extremely long-lived; certainly one of Italy's least-known, but finest red wines. Serve it with your finest beef roast!

VENETO

(VAY-nay-toh)   Known as Venetia for centuries and our name for it — a Region of 7098 square miles in area, about 4½ million in population; the Capitol is Venice (Venezia in Italian — this *is* confusing); the Region is rich in history, art and architecture. The name stems from the ancient people — the Veneti; conquered by the Romans in the 2nd Century BC; its history is really the history of the City — the strong City-State, the Republic that ruled the sea lanes after defeating Genoa, etc.; at one time extending west almost to Piedmont and S to Albania; its present boundaries were formed in 1947; its neighbor on the N is mostly Trentino-Alto Adige Region, on the E is Fruili-Venezia Giulia (these three Regions comprise what is often referred to as "Tre-Venezie"); on the S is the Adriatic Sea and Emilia-Romagna and on the W is Lombardy Region. It is the home of some of the best mountain resorts in Italy and the world-famous seaside resort — the Lido — in Venice. Wines have been made here since the Romans — in the Verona area (Bardolino, Soave, Valpolicella), Colli Euganei, Breganze and Piave areas; the average annual production is close to one billion liters.

VENETO REGION

VENEZIA

(vay-NAY-tzee-ah)   Venice to us — a city of 100,000 people, Capitol of Veneto Region, actually built on a lagoon off the Coast; famous resort city and tourist stop for centuries with its famous buildings and canals.

VERDECA

(vair-DAY-ka)   Ordinary white wine grape grown in Puglia Region; used in Locorotondo, Martinafranca, Vermouth and Verdeca Di Alberobello.

VERDELLO

(vair-DEL-lo)   Excellent white wine grape grown in the Umbria Region, an important part of Orvieto wine (see).

VERDICCHIO

(vair-DEEK-kee-oh)   Excellent white wine grape grown in the Marche Region, the informing grape in the next entry:

VERDICCHIO DEI CASTELLI DI IESI

(vair-DEEK-kee-oh day kahs-TEL-lee dee YAY-see)   **DOC**   One of Italy's best-known wines made in and near the town of Iesi (Jesi on export labels) in the Marche Region; it is 80% Verdicchio and 20% either Trebbiano or Malvasia grapes; dry, slightly yellow, best drunk young — a superb wine with fish. The bottle used is reminiscent of an amphora, supposedly to show its early origin in the days when all wines were kept in amphora-shaped vessels. There is a *classico* zone which produces most of it and a *spumante* is available; annual production is over ten million liters; avoid it if three years old.

VERDICCHIO DI MATELICA

(vair-DEEK-kee-oh dee mah-TAY-lee-ka)   **DOC**   A very close "cousin" to the one above, from the same grape formula, but outside the *classico* zone and near the town of Matelica; it is frequently drier than the Iesi wine and a *spumante* is also made here. Annual production is over 500,000 liters.

VERDISO

(vair-DEE-so)   Ordinary white wine grape grown in Veneto Region.

VERDUZZO

(vair-DOOTZ-tzoh)   Good white wine grape grown in Friuli-Venezia Giulia and Veneto Regions; the wine made from it is not distinctive except for a sweeter version known as Verduzzo Di Ramandolo — a good dessert wine. See Colli Orientali and Vini Del Piave.

VERMENTINO

(vair-MAYN-tee-no) Excellent white wine grape formerly heavily grown in Liguria Region; the wines it produces are dry, fresh-tasting, medium-bodied, excellent with fish with its slightly bitter after-taste. It has recently been transplanted to Sardinia Region and is adapting very well.

VERMENTINO DI GALLURA

(vair-MAYN-tee-no dee gahl-LOO-ra) **DOC** This wine is made from 95% Vermentino grapes on the Gallura peninsula at the N end of Sardinia Island (Region); gold in color, dry, strong (15% +), a *superiore* is available; about 300,000 liters made annually.

VERMOUTH

(vair-MOOTH) Not to be overlooked, but books have been written on this wine; in review, the recipe was created by an Italian, it has been religiously copied by others, it comes both light and dark (dry and sweet), its home is Turin in the Piedmont Region, and the annual production is over 100 million liters! Have you ever tried 50-50 dry and sweet on the rocks?

VERNACCIA

(vair-NACH-chee-ah) Normally a white wine grape grown (1) in Liguria and used in Vernaccia Di Corniglia; (2) in Marche Region and used in Vernaccia Di Serrapetrona; (3) in Tuscany Region and used in Vernaccia Di San Gimignano; and (4) in Sardinia Region, used in Vernaccia Di Oristano. Each one is said to be a slightly different variety!! There is also a dark variety grown on Sicily — Vernaccia Nera!

VERNACCIA DI CANNARA

(vair-NACH-chee-ah dee kahn-NAHR-ah) is a sweet red wine made in Umbria Region from a grape called the Cometta (just to confuse the issue even more)!!

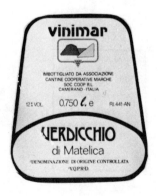

VERNACCIA DI CORNIGLIA

(vair-NACH-chee-ah dee kor-NEE-lee-ah)   is a white wine from Corniglia (one of the "five lands" of Cinqueterra [see]) in the Liguria Region.

VERNACCIA DI ORISTANO

(vair-NACH-chee-ah dee or-ee-STAH-noh)   **DOC**   A white wine from the Vernaccia grape and Oristano, a small town near Cagliari, Sardinia Region; the wine is golden in color, dry, strong (15% +), rich, rounded, full-bodied, with two years of age required before release; with another year, a *superiore*, with four years a *riserva* and it will often improve until its tenth birthday; a *liquoroso* at 16% is made and requires another two years in wood; also a *liquoroso secco* at 18% is made; this wine makes an excellent aperitif when chilled and the sweeter version is good as a dessert wine.

VERNACCIA DI SAN GIMIGNANO

(vair-NACH-chee-ah dee SAHN JEE-meen-YAH-no)   **DOC**   An excellent and famous wine from the Vernaccia grape grown on the hillsides of the town of San Gimignano — the city of towers — between Florence and Siena in Tuscany Region; it is pale to deep-gold, aromatic, dry, better with age, a *riserva* with one year; a *liquoroso* is also made. The average annual production is three million liters. This wine was the first granted DOC status-on June 5, 1966. Its history goes back to the 12th century and it is good with both light and dark meats. Candidate for DOCG.

VERNACCIA DI SERRAPETRONA

(vair-NACH-chee-ah dee sair-ra-pay-TROH-na)   **DOC**   The town of Serra-petrona makes this red wine from 80% Vernaccia and 20% Sangiovese/ Montepulciano/Ciliegiolo grapes — a sweet, red, *spumante*!! It is strong (17%), and the partially-dried grapes make it either a *dolce* or *amabile*; it will not please many wine-lovers but it has been made and consumed here for centuries!!

VERONA

(vay-ROH-na)   (1)   City in the W part of Veneto Region built on an Etruscan town;   (2)   famous as the home of Romeo and Juliet and (3)   Bardolino, Soave and Valpolicella; there is a tremendous amount of Verona Bianco and Verona Rosso made.

VESPAIOLO

(vays-PAH-yo-lo)   White wine grape grown in the Veneto Region.

VESPOLINA

(vays-poh-LEE-nah)   Good red wine grape grown in Piedmont Region and used there with the Nebbiolo grape in Boca, Fara and Ghemme; also used with the Barbera grape in Lombardy Region.

VESUVIO

(vay-SOO-vee-oh)   is what we call Mt. Vesuvius — the active volcano just S of Naples, Campania Region, and a strong part of that skyline with its present height of 4200 feet; there is a railroad going almost to the top. Pliny the Elder died while investigating the famous eruption of 79 AD, which buried Pompeii and Herculaneum; major eruptions recently were 1906 and 1945; a serious earthquake in November 1980 did much damage to excavated portions of Pompeii; the lower slopes are very fertile from the volcanic ash and the constantly re-planted vineyards produce much wine. See Lacrima Christi del Vesuvio.

VESUVIO is the name of a DOC zone that was supposed to have been approved some time ago but the latest list dated July 1, 1981, from the DOC Committee in Rome did not include it. Sources say that it should be approved in time for the 1981 harvest; there are:

BIANCO

(bee-AHN-koh)   is a white wine from a minimum of 50% Verdeca, minimum of 30% Coda Di Volpe with Falanghina and Greco grapes; pale-yellow to straw-colored, dry, good "quaffing" wine, light to medium-bodied; under certain conditions it may be called Lacrima Christi del Vesuvio; there is a *spumante naturale* and a *liquoroso*.

ROSATO

(roh-SAH-toh)   is a good rosé, light-bodied to medium-bodied, dry, and made from Piedirosso/Sciascinoso/Aglianico grapes.

ROSSO

(ROHS-soh)   is made from a minimum of 40% Piedirosso, a maximum of 40% Sciascinoso and 20% Aglianico grapes; ruby-red, dry, medium-bodied. Both the *Rosato* and the *Rosso* may be, under certain conditions, labeled Lacrima Christi Del Vesuvio.

VIEN DE NUS

(vee-en de NOOS)   An intense red wine from the Petit Rouge/Dolcetto grapes made in the village of Nus just E of Aosta in the Valle D'Aosta Region; dry, rich, full-bodied, one year of age is required and much better with three or so, candidate for DOC.

VIGNA

(VEEN-ay)   Vineyard.

VIGNANELLO

(veen-yah-NEL-lo)   Small town N of Rome, Lazio Region, producing a good dry red wine from Sangiovese and other grapes.

VIGNETO

(veen-YAY-toh)   is the Italian equivalent of the French word "cru" which may not appear on Italian wine labels — an ECM ruling. At this time, there is no system in Italy for rating vineyards such as the French have done.

VIN D'ARNAD ET MONTJOVET

(Fr: vehn dahr-NAH-day mawn-joh-VAY)   Superior red wines from these two towns and Issogne in the Valle D'Aosta Region; the Nebbiolo is the principal grape but Neyret/Freisa and others may be included; dry, full-bodied, brilliant red, better with at least two years of age.

VIN D'ISSOGNE

(vehn dee-SOHN-ya)   See above entry.

VIN DU CONSEIL

(Fr: vehn dew kawn-SAY-ya)   Excellent white wine from the Petite Arvine grape made at the Ag School in Aosta, the Valle D'Aosta Region.

VIN RUSPO

(veen ROO-spoh)   From Carmignano (see) in Tuscany Region, the name means "stolen" and refers to an old custom of the sharecroppers. It is from the Chianti (see) grapes and made as a rosé each December and really belongs in the *vini novelli* class of wines (see). The grapes are Sangiovese/Canaiolo/Cabernet Sauvignon/Trebbiano/Malvasia.

VIN SANTO or **VINO SANTO**

(veen SAHN-toh)   A strong, sweet dessert wine made all over Italy by many producers using many combinations of grapes and each claiming to be the one and only TRUE one! The grapes are allowed to "raisin" for several months, then made into wine generally kept in the attic for several years, "sleeping" in the winter and "working" in the summer, then filtered and bottled; the result is usually a very complex dessert wine; if allowed to age still more, it often loses some of its sweetness. The name is translated "wine of the Saints" or "Saint's wine" and one story insists that it is due to the wine being made during Easter or Holy Week; there are several others!

VIN SANTO DI GAMBELLARA

(veen SAHN-toh dee gahm-bel-LAHR-ah) **DOC** This "Saint's wine" is made in the town of Gambellara in the Veneto Region from the same grapes as the Gambellara wine is made — 80-90% Garganega and the rest Trebbiano; deep amber in color, sweet and smooth, two years of age is required; see Gambellara.

VIN SANTO TRENTINO

See Trentino.

VIN SANTO TOSCANA

(veen SAHN-toh toh-SKAH-na) There are many producers, each with his own version of this wine in the Tuscany Region; they vary from 15% to 19% alcohol, made in the usual manner; most of them are smooth and sweet but drier versions do exist; generally at their best from five to ten years of age. Candidate for DOC.

VINI DEI CASTELLI ROMANI

See Castelli Romani.

VINI DEL PIAVE or PIAVE

(vee-nee del pee-AHV-a)   **DOC**   The Piave River rises in the Alps and flows S through the Veneto Region into the Adriatic some 20 miles N of Venice; the area from Conegliano to the mouth of the river is the DOC area. Labels may read "Vini del Piave" followed by the variety of the grape, or "(variety) del Piave," or "Piave (variety)." There are four wines as listed, but it has been requested that the following wines be included in the DOC: Pinot Bianco, Pinot Grigio, Pinot Nero and Raboso; they may be approved in 1981.

CABERNET

(kah-bear-NAY)   is made from either the Cabernet Franc or the Cabernet Sauvignon; ruby-red turning to the garnet shade with age, dry, full-bodied, a *riserva* with three years, peaks about six; serve with your best beef roast!

MERLOT

(mair-LOW)   must be made with 90% Merlot grapes and is a typical soft, smooth, ruby-red, dry wine from this grape; it may be labeled *vecchio* with two years of age, but drink it before it reaches its fifth birthday.

TOCAI

(toh-KIE)   is from 95% of this grape; light yellow with a greenish tint, dry, fresh, an excellent carafe wine.

VERDUZZO

(vair-DOOTZ-tzoh)   is a pale-yellow, dry, medium-bodied wine from this grape; drink it young.

VINI ITALIANI
(vee-nee ee-tahl-lee-AH-nee)   Italian wines.

VINI NOVELLI
(VEE-nee noh-VEL-lee)   Translated "new wines" — such as the Beaujolais Nouveau with which all are familiar. Many wines are made this way — Bardolino, Nebbiolo, Pinot Nero, to name three, and from many Regions. As in all wines made in this manner, they have a low alcoholic content, are semi-dry, with a very pleasant fruity taste and must be consumed within a few months of the harvest, probably before the next April. Perhaps they should be classified as a "fun thing" as a bottle of good mature wine can be purchased for about the same price. Because of their perishable nature, it is doubtful if they will be found in America.

VINI TIPICI
(vee-nee TEE-pee-chee)   translates as "typical wines" — a more or less meaningless term. See DOC for its inclusion as a category under that law.

VINO — VINI
(VEE-no + VEE-nee)   Wine and the plural — wines.

VINO RUVIDO
(VEE-no ROO-vee-doh)   A coarse or rough wine.

VINO DA TAGLIO
(VEE-no da TAHL-yo)   A wine possessing certain characteristics of color, body or strength, making it valuable to add to a lesser wine lacking those qualities — a very necessary part of the winemaker's art. Many Italian growers have pronounced that there is more Italian wine in some French wines than there is French!!

VINO DA TAVOLA
(VEE-no da TAH-voh-la)   Wine for the table — or table wine. See DOC for fuller explanation under that law.

VINO DELLE PERINE

(VEE-no del-la pay-REE-na) Red wine from Sangiovese/Trebbiano/
Vermentino/Moscato grapes made in Liguria Region; deep red, soft, smooth,
semi-dry, can be strong (13½%), drink it fairly young.

VINO DI LUSSO

(VEE-no dee LOOS-so) A very special wine of deluxe quality.

VINO NOBILE DI MONTEPULCIANO

(VEE-no NOH-bee-lay dee mohn-tee-pool-CHAH-no) **DOC and DOCG**
One of Italy's top wines — for the connoisseur — made from 50-70% Sangiovese (Prugnolo), 10-20% Canaiolo, 10-20% Malvasia/Trebbiano and a maximum of 8% Grechetto/Mammolo grapes, in the town of Montepulciano, SE
of Siena in Tuscany Region; tannic when young; it is dry, soft and elegant
with proper age; two years in wood is required before sale, a *riserva* with three
years and a *riserva speciale* with four or more years; better by far with ten
years, and good for another ten or twenty!!

VINO NOSTRANO

(VEE-no no-STRAH-no) A local wine.

VINUCOLO

(VEE-noo-KOH-loh) A weak wine.

VITERBO

(vee-TAIR-bo) Small town N of Rome, Lazio Region, once the residence of
the Popes; a white wine area.

VITIGNO

(vee-TEEN-yoh) Grape vine variety.

VITULANO

(vee-too-LAH-no) Ordinary red, dry wine made in the Campania Region,
probably with Sangiovese grapes.

Vino Nobile

di

Montepulciano

DENOMINAZIONE DI ORIGINE CONTROLLATA

W X Y

These letters are used only at the beginning of certain foreign words and symbols and are not part of the Italian alphabet.

WEISSBURGUNDER
German name used in the Alto Adige area for the Pinot Bianco (Pinot Blanc) grape.

WELSCHRIESLING
German name used in the Alto Adige area for the Riesling Italico grape.

WHITE CHIANTI
(kee-AHN-tee)   Since DOC defines Chianti as a *red* wine, this name may no longer be used. With a glut of white wine grapes in the Tuscany Region, there has been some agitation to renew the name; it is unlikely that it will be accomplished. White Chianti was generally made from the Trebbiano/ Malvasia and other grapes. See Bianco Della Lega and Galestro for current information.

WINE GRAPE VARIETIES
This alphabetical list of wine grapes grown in Italy indicates the great number of varieties as given in the *disciplinari* and from the growers. It is not intended to be complete, nor to indicate sub-varieties or synonyms; that is a separate field — for the scholars or botanists and their ampelographies, of which there are several. These are presented as a matter of information. The letter following the name indicates a red or white grape.

A

Abbuoto	r	Alessano	w
Aglianico	r	Alicanta	r
Albana	w	Ancellotta	r
Albanello	w	Ansonica	w
Albarola	w	Arneis	w
Aleatico	r	Asprinio	w

Z

ZABAGLIONE

(ZAH-bah-lee-OH-nay)   A very fine custard dessert made with eggs, TLC, and Marsala; a fitting dessert for a fine wine dinner (and a favorite of the author).

ZAGAROLO

(zah-gah-ROH-loh)   **DOC**   Small town SE of Rome, Lazio Region, producing a good, light carafe wine from a maximum of 70% Malvasia, minimum of 30% Trebbiano and to 10% Bellone/Bonvino grapes; made both *secco* and *amabile*; there is a *superiore* available; the *secco* is preferred.

ZIANO

(tzee-AH-no)   A small town W of Piacenza in the W tip of Emilia-Romagna Region; this area produces Gutturnio Dei Colli Piacentini (see) a DOC wine; the entire area is being promoted for a zone and these wines are listed as candidates for DOC: Barbera, Bonarda (*dolce* and *frizzante*), Malvasia (*dolce* and *frizzante*) and Pinot Grigio.

ZIBIBBO

(tzee-BEEB-bo)   White wine grape of the Muscat family grown on the island of Pantelleria, S of Sicily Region.

ZUCCHERO

(tzook-KAY-roh)   Sugar. ECM prohibits sugaring of Italian wines, while allowing it in French and German wines. (It is also prohibited in California wines.)

ZUCCO

(TZOOK-ko)   Small town in Sicily Region producing the wine — Moscato Di Zucco (see).

D.O.C. WINES BY REGION

The first wine was approved on May 5, 1966. This list is accurate through July 1, 1981.

ABRUZZO REGION
Montepulciano D'Abruzzo
Trebbiano D'Abruzzo

BASILICATA REGION
Aglianico Del Vulture

CALABRIA REGION
Ciro
Donnici
Greco Di Bianco
Lamezia
Melissa
Pollino
Sant'Anna di Isola Capo Rizzuto
Savuto

CAMPANIA REGION
Capri
Fiano D'Avellino
Greco Di Tufo
Ischia
Solopaca
Taurasi

EMILIA – ROMAGNA REGION
Albana Di Romagna — also DOCG
Bianco Di Scandiano
*Colli Bolognesi
Gutturnio Dei Colli Piacentini
Lambrusco Di Sorbara
Lambrusco Grasparossa Di Castelvetro
Lambrusco Reggiano
Lambrusco Salamino Di Santa Croce

*Several different wines are included in this D.O.C. zone

Monterosso Val D'Arda
Sangiovese Di Romagna
Trebbianino Val Trebbia
Trebbiano Di Romagna

FRIULI – VENEZIA GIULIA REGION

*Aquileia
*Colli Orientali Del Friuli
*Collio Goriziano
*Grave Del Friuli
*Isonzo
*Latisana

LAZIO REGION

Aleatico Di Gradoli
Bianco Capena
Cerveteri
Cesanese Del Piglio
Cesanese Di Affile
Cesanese Di Olevano – Romano
Colli Albani
Colli Lanuvini
Cori
Est! Est!! Est!!!
Frascati
Marino Bianco
Merlot Di Aprilia
Montecompatri – Colonna
Sangiovese Di Aprilia
Trebbiano Di Aprilia
Velletri
Zagarolo

LIGURIA REGION

Cinqueterre
Rossese Di Dolceacqua

LOMBARDY REGION

Botticino
Capriano del Colle
Cellatica
Colli Morenici Mantovani Del Garda
Franciacorta
Lugana

*Several different wines are included in this D.O.C. zone

LOMBARDY – *continued*

*Oltrepò Pavese
Riviera Del Garda Bresciano
Tocai Di San Martino Della Battaglia
Valcalepio
Valtellina
Valtellina Superiore

MARCHE REGION

Bianchello Del Matauro
Bianco Dei Colli Maceratesi
Falerio Dei Colli Ascolani
Rosso Conero
Rosso Piceno
Sangiovese Dei Colli Pesaresi
Verdicchio Dei Castelli Di Iesi
Verdicchio Di Matelica
Vernaccia Di Serrapetrona

MOLISE REGION

–

PIEDMONT REGION

Asti Spumante
Barbaresco -- *also DOCG*
Barbera D'Alba
Barbera D'Asti
Barbera Del Monferrato
Barolo – also DOCG
Boca
Brachettto D'Acqui
Bramaterra
Carema
Colli Tortonesi
Cortese Dell'Alto Monferrato
Dolcetto D'Acqui
Dolcetto D'Alba
Dolcetto D'Asti
Dolcetto Delle Langhe Monregalesi
Dolcetto Di Diano D'Alba
Dolcetto Di Dogliani
Dolcetto D'Ovada

*Several different wines are included in this D.O.C. zone

Erbaluce Di Caluso
Fara
Freisa D'Asti
Freisa Di Chieri
Gattinara
Gavi
Ghemme
Grignolino D'Asti
Grignolino Del Monferrato Casalese
Lessona
Malvasia Di Casorzo D'Asti
Malvasia Di Castelnuovo Don Bosco
Moscato D'Asti
Moscato Naturale D'Asti
Nebbiolo D'Alba
Rubino Di Cantavenna
Sizzano

PUGLIA REGION

Aleatico Di Puglia
Brindisi
Cacc'e Mmitte Di Lucera
Castel Del Monte
Copertino
Leverano
Locorotondo
Martinafranca
Matino
Moscato Di Trani
Ostuni
Primitivo Di Manduria
Rosso Barletta
Rosso Canosa
Rosso Di Cerignola
Salice Salento
San Severo
Squinzano

SARDINIA REGION
Campidano Di Terralba
Cannonau Di Sardegna
Carignano Del Sulcis
Giro Di Cagliari
Malvasia Di Bosa
Malvasia Di Cagliari
Mandrolisai
Monica Di Cagliari
Monica Di Sardegna
Moscato Di Cagliari
Moscato Di Sardegna Spumante
Moscato Di Sorso—Sennori
Nasco Di Cagliari
Nuragus Di Cagliari
Vermentino Di Gallura
Vernaccia Di Oristano

SICILY REGION
Bianco Alcamo
Cerasuolo Di Vittoria
Etna
Faro
Malvasia Delle Lipari
Marsala
Moscato Di Noto
Moscato Di Pantelleria
Moscato Di Siracusa
Moscato Passito Di Pantelleria

TRENTINO—ALTO ADIGE REGION
*Alto Adige
Caldaro
Casteller
Colli Di Bolzano
Meranese Di Collina
Santa Maddelena
Sorni
*Terlano
Teroldego Rotaliano
*Trentino
Valdadige
*Valle Isarco

*Several different wines are included in this D.O.C. zone

TUSCANY REGION
Bianco Della Valdinievole
Bianco Di Pitigliano
Bianco Pisane Di San Torpe
Bianco Vergine Val Di Chiana
Brunello Di Montalcino — also DOCG
Carmignano
Chianti
Elba
Montecarlo Bianco
Montescudaio
Morello Di Scansano
Parrina
Rosso Della Colline Lucchesi
Vernaccia Di San Gimignano
Vino Nobile Di Montepulciano — also DOCG
UMBRIA REGION
Colli Altotiberini
Colli Del Trasimeno
Montefalco
Orvieto
Torgiano
VALLE D'AOSTA REGION
Donnaz
Enfer D'Arviers
VENETO REGION
Bardolino
Bianco Di Custoza
*Breganze
Cabernet Di Pramaggiore
*Colli Berici
*Colli Euganei
Gambellara
Merlot Di Pramaggiore
*Montello e Colli Asolani
Prosecco Di Conegliano—Valdobbiadene
Soave
Tocai Di Lison
Valpolicella
*Vini Del Piave

*Several different wines are included in this D.O.C. zone

ADMINISTRATIVE REGIONS OF ITALY

Area in square miles		Population	
Sicily	9831	Lombardy	8,500,000
Sardinia	9196	Lazio	5,000,000
Lombardy	9190	Sicily	5,000,000
Piedmont	9187	Campania	4,700,000
Tuscany	8876	Veneto	4,500,000
Emilia-Romagna	8542	Piedmont	4,500,000
Puglia	7469	Emilia-Romagna	4,000,000
Veneto	7098	Puglia	4,000,000
Lazio	6480	Tuscany	3,500,000
Calabria	5823	Liguria	2,000,000
Trentino-Alto Adige	5252	Calabria	2,000,000
Campania	5214	Trentino-Alto Adige	1,900,000
Abruzzo	4468	Marche	1,500,000
Basilicata	3856	Sardinia	1,500,000
Marche	3744	Friuli-Venezia Giulia	1,300,000
Umbria	3270	Abruzzo	1,250,000
Friuli-Venezia Giulia	2948	Umbria	800,000
Liguria	2098	Basilicata	580,000
Molise	1334	Molise	330,000
Valle D'Aosta	1260	Valle D'Aosta	125,000

Notes

Notes

Notes

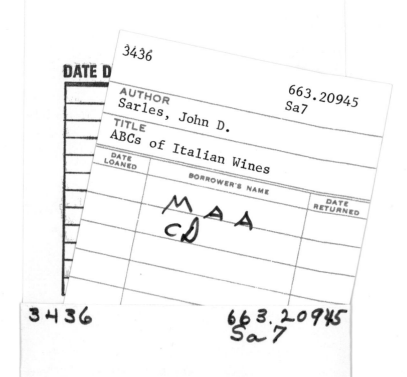